THE **Principal**
AS **Technology Leader**

Theodore Creighton

CORWIN PRESS, INC.
A Sage Publications Company
Thousand Oaks, California

For information:

Corwin Press, Inc.
A Sage Publications Company
2455 Teller Road
Thousand Oaks, California 91320
www.corwinpress.com

Sage Publications Ltd.
6 Bonhill Street
London EC2A 4PU
United Kingdom

Sage Publications India Pvt. Ltd.
B-42 Panchsheel Enclave
New Delhi 110 017 India

Printed in the United States of America

Library of Congress Cataloging-in-Publication Data

Creighton, Theodore B.
The principal as technology leader / Theodore Creighton.
    p. cm.
Includes bibliographical references and index.
ISBN 0-7619-4541-5 (C) — ISBN 0-7619-4542-3 (P)
    1. Educational technology—Planning. 2. Educational leadership.
3. School principals. I. Title.
LB1028.3 .C74 2003
371.2′012—dc21

                                        2002010061

This book is printed on acid-free paper.

02 03 04 05 06 10 9 8 7 6 5 4 3 2 1

Acquisitions Editor:	Robert D. Clouse
Associate Editor:	Kristen Gibson
Editorial Assistant:	Erin Clow
Copy Editor:	Teresa Herlinger
Production Editor:	Diane S. Foster
Typesetter:	C&M Digitals (P) Ltd
Proofreader:	Scott Oney
Indexer:	Molly Hall
Cover Designer:	Michael Dubowe
Production Artist:	Janet Foulger

Contents

Preface

Current research indicates that schools with effective technology curricula also have strong administrative leadership supporting and sustaining technology programs for both teachers and students (Office of Technology Assessment, 1995; Richie, 1996; Richie & Rodriguez, 1997). The Office of Technology Assessment (OTA) has found that well-informed administrators who are comfortable and competent using technology have been key players in leading and supporting technology in schools (OTA, 1988, 1989, 1995).

Much evidence exists (Lemke, 1998) suggesting that technology programs in schools operate at a minimal level (e.g., they are set up to do word processing and spreadsheets). Although all states require administrators to take courses in leadership, management, and the challenges of special education, few require (or even expect) administrators to be technologically competent (Richie & Rodriguez, 1997).

Moss Kanter (2001) argues the following:

Too often, new technologies have been used to kill time instead of teach better. Too often, technology (e.g., software) has promoted glitz, glamour, and graphics instead of serious learning. Too often, the Internet has promoted the *surfing culture* where users click their way across an ocean of information, feeling overwhelmed by the vastness of it all and never dipping below the surface. (p. 68)

The author believes the problem relates to a misguided focus on technology as hardware and software. What's needed is a conceptual knowledge of how technologies can restructure education and improve instruction and achievement for our nation's students.

A pervasive need exists for a book to help school administrators and other school leaders plan and manage for the use of technology in educational settings with student learning and teacher development as the driving forces.

KNOWLEDGE BASE

Studies show that school administrators' training and knowledge base have not kept pace with the rapid changes in both education and technology, causing a lack of authentic support for the integration and implementation of technology beyond a basic level. In addition to providing a knowledge base beyond the basic level, this book will focus on several key questions such as the following:

1. If certain weaknesses or deficiencies are prevalent related to technology and school leadership, how does the principal or other educational leader correct such deficiencies?

2. How does the educational leader effectively manage and integrate technology programs throughout the entire school curriculum (beyond the traditional core subjects)?

3. What does the educational community really mean by *supporting technology*? What do we mean when we say that our school has an effective technology program?

4. What strategies can principals use to see that teachers and students develop *technology fluency* and to navigate their way around the chaotic environment we call the Web? How do we analyze, synthesize, and evaluate the enormous amount of data—and turn those data into information and that information into wisdom (Lemke, 1998).

My intention is to provide a very detailed and comprehensive explanation and specific plan designed to help school principals and other educational leaders become managers and facilitators of successful and appropriate use of technology in our schools. This approach focuses on applicable and relevant professional development programs for teachers that in turn will affect student achievement.

The predominance of traditional instructional modes should be a concern for those who seek improvement. This tradition in instruction is particularly problematic in a field that purports to emphasize *educational leadership* (Murphy, 1997). The author will offer innovative alternatives (based on research and practice) to the traditional instructional modes shown to have a positive impact on student learning in the area of technology.

WHAT THIS BOOK IS NOT ABOUT

You will not find discussion of technology hardware and software in this book. Not only do we already have a plethora of books and workbooks on these components of technology, but my argument is that our overemphasis on hardware and software is exactly the cause of our current problem. It's the reason our critics say that technology use in our schools has not yet moved from promise to practice, and why our technology programs still focus and operate at a minimal level (Cuban, 2001).

Instead of focusing on "the boxes and wires," this book will look closely at other issues: (a) How do we use technology to improve student achievement? (b) How do administrators promote technology as a tool for collaboration as well as stimulation for real, authentic learning experiences that allow for far greater student achievement than ever before? and (c) How do we as technology leaders design and implement effective staff development programs for teachers?

LIPSTICK ON A BULLDOG

Rosebeth Moss Kanter (2001), distinguished author and professor from the Harvard Business School, uses the above metaphor to point to businesses mistakenly assuming they are using technology such as the Internet and Web pages in highly productive ways. She contends that the way many "wannadotcoms" conduct business through the World Wide Web may be likened to "putting lipstick on a bulldog" (p. 72). This kind of makeup job is hard to do and does not work. The bulldog doesn't suddenly become beautiful because it is forced to wear lipstick. Nothing else about the bulldog or its behavior has changed. And the use of cosmetics just covers up problems that still exist under the makeup. "Putting lipstick on a bulldog won't transform enough. Nothing about the bulldog or its behavior has changed. Makeup can't hide everything: change takes deeper stuff" (p. vii). For example, many schools are guilty of *putting up a Web site or two*, and *investing in fancy hardware and software*, thinking they are technologically advanced.

I argue that we have a similar situation existing in many of our schools regarding the use of technology. The implementation of hardware and software merely brings about cosmetic changes to our schools, with little evidence of influencing teaching and learning in meaningful and systemic ways. A company is not transformed simply because it creates a Web site; schools are not transformed simply by the purchase and installation of computers, CD burners, and Internet access.

Required is a more complete, in-depth makeover—specifically, educational leaders who can manage and plan differently for the use of technology in educational settings. Moss Kanter is right: Technology is a great facilitator, but it is not a substitute for the rich interaction between teacher and student. The evidence is pretty clear: When students are in student-centered, student-directed, collaborative classrooms supported by rich social discourse and authentic tasks, they learn more (Nicaise & Barnes, 1996).

Don't misunderstand me. I believe strongly that the use of technology in our schools has the potential for significant and radical educational reform. But only if we get beyond the cosmetic changes of fancy computer labs and slick Web pages. Much evidence also exists indicating technology has not radically changed the way teachers teach; instead, most technology mirrors traditional instructional pedagogy. And much worse, examples abound showing that technology in the classroom can be used as a disguise for poor teaching. Herein lies the importance of the principal as technology leader: The principal must make certain we constantly strive to improve teaching and learning. The focus must move beyond the cosmetic changes of fancy boxes and wires and toward the use of technology to enhance and advance what we already know about effective teaching.

SO, WHAT IS THIS BOOK ABOUT?

It will not be the computer alone that will affect teaching and learning, but a change in pedagogical thinking toward student-centered classrooms with lots of constructivist, project-based activities, with opportunities for social discourse and collaboration between teacher and student, and student and student. Exemplary teaching must accompany technology in the classroom in order for it to be used effectively.

First of all, I confess that I will discuss such traditional issues as strategic planning for technology and designing effective staff development programs. And yes, I will talk about how principals can manage, lead, and sustain effective technology implementation. Certainly, some discussion on teacher evaluation and the use of technology must also be included.

But equally important, though usually not presented in formal university principal (or teacher) preparation programs, is how to deal with teachers and others resistant to technology implementation. How does the principal as technology leader deal with the *saboteurs* and *resisters* present in our ranks? In our profession, we talk much about what effective programs look like, but what do ineffective programs look like? In other words, why do technology programs fail? Are schools really doing all they can do to see that technology is used to truly enhance better teaching and learning?

The final chapter "puts it all together" and presents a model of technology implementation. This technology initiative is a university/public school collaborative and specifically targets the use of technology to assist minority students and others with special learning needs. The purpose of this last chapter is to move beyond the "why" of the problem and directly address the "how" for principals and other school leaders.

ACKNOWLEDGMENTS

Someone once said that an author is essentially the pen through which significant others write. Allow me to share these significant others with my readers.

First of all, I am fortunate to have as a colleague Genevieve Brown, a fellow professor and department chair at Sam Houston State University. Those of you who have experience in higher education know how important climate and culture are to the professor. Through her leadership, the SHSU culture not only encourages and supports an individual's writing and research, but also values one's work as an important contribution to the education community. Genevieve, though your name does not appear as a contributing author, your influence, both professional and personal, weaves through much of my writing.

I must also mention my thanks to the many aspiring and practicing principals I've worked with in four states, who have dared to challenge the status quo. In decades past, maintaining the status quo was appropriate. Today, with the fast-paced change of technology, a different leader is required. I've met principals as technology leaders who accept this challenge and who insist on keeping teaching and learning as the driving forces in their leadership. Your commitment to children and teachers has sustained my writing and my belief that individual principals are at the core of education reform.

The last significant other is really first. My wife, Linda, has spent countless hours as the major editor of my work. And her editing does not take place during normal working hours—most is done in the early mornings and late evenings, sandwiched between events in her already busy day. My newest idea involves a book entitled *The Stresses of an Author's Spouse.*

The contributions of the following reviewers are also gratefully acknowledged:

Kim Randall
  Teacher
  Claremont Academy and ECC
  Arlington, VA

John Burl Artis
  Assistant Superintendent
  Upper Arlington City Schools
  Upper Arlington, OH

Kim Leblanc
    Technology Resource Specialist
    Cakasieu Parish Public Schools
    Lake Charles, LA

Vicki Barnett
    Instructor
    ITT Technical Institute
    Tampa, FL

About the Author

Theodore B. Creighton is currently a Professor at the Center for Research and Doctoral Studies in Educational Leadership at Sam Houston State University, where he teaches courses in educational research, educational statistics, and program evaluation. He previously served as Coordinator of the Principal Preparation Program at Idaho State University, where he taught courses in the principalship, change strategies, and school personnel. While at Idaho State University, he was Director of the Idaho Administrative Technology Leadership Center, a collaborative university/public school partnership that provided technology training to school administrators in 55 school districts in Eastern Idaho. His background includes teaching at various grade levels in Washington, D.C.; Cleveland; and Los Angeles. His administrative experience includes serving as principal and superintendent in both Fresno and Kern Counties, California. He holds a B.S. in teacher education from Indiana University of Pennsylvania, master's degrees in educational administration from Kent State University and California State University, Long Beach, and an Ed.D. from the University of California, Davis/Fresno State University joint doctoral program.

Creighton is currently the Executive Director of the National Council of Professors of Educational Administration (NCPEA) and serves on the National Commission for the Advancement of Educational Leadership Programs (NCAELP). He is widely published in educational leadership journals, and is the author of the best-seller *Schools and Data: The Educator's Guide for Using Data to Improve Decision Making*. His current research focuses on recruitment and selection procedures in university preparation programs.

CHAPTER ONE

Principal Leadership and Successful Technology Implementation

Some (including this author) might argue that perhaps school leadership as practiced by today's principal is outdated unless it helps faculty address the great challenges presented by the introduction of technology in our schools. Before you put down my book, let me state that the principal is not really to blame: University principal preparation programs are not adequately providing the necessary skills and dispositions required of principals in this recent new role. Granted, university programs and state credentialing agencies require a basic skill level in the use of technology before principal certification is granted. Though I agree that basic skills in the use of technology (word processing, spreadsheet and database use) are important, this book is not about hardware and software. The theme of this book is that effective integration of technology has more to do with teaching pedagogy, and very little to do with technology itself. The author further contends that in too many schools, we see the use of "technology" with an absence of relationship to instructional objectives and learning outcomes.

A principal's mission must now include designing and implementing new strategies to help teachers recognize, understand, and integrate technology with teaching and learning in the classroom. The mere presence of hardware and software in the classroom does not assure meaningful learning for students. We are beyond the point of deciding whether or not we will accept technology in our schools. The crucial task at hand now is to decide how to implement this technology effectively into instruction.

As if our profession needs a new buzz-word, researchers and current writers on leadership have coined the term *e-leadership* (Avolio, 2000; Moss Kanter, 2001; Quinn-Mills, 2001). Harvard Business School professor Quinn-Mills contends that the core of e-leadership "requires leaders to identify those who are expert in the new technology and support them, even stepping out of the way if necessary—and let new people point the direction giving them initiative—and to build an organizational framework (positions and culture) in which the new can displace the old" (p. v).

Avolio (2000) discusses the relationship between leadership and technology and suggests that leaders must play a more proactive role in implementing technology, and more specifically, strive to interface the human and information technology components. Many point to the problem of overemphasis on the technological aspect at the exclusion of the human resource function. Avolio warns of the creation of "information junkyards" (p. 4). The essence of e-leadership is to produce a change in attitudes, feelings, thinking, behavior, and performance with individuals.

To carry off this improvement in technology implementation, principals must be willing to alter existing leadership practices evidenced in most schools; and they must also be open to the probability of participating in a transformation of traditional leadership skills, knowledge, and dispositions. Existing research, as quoted throughout this book, reveals that the use of technology in our schools exists at a minimal or basic level, at best. Even the best of schools have barely tapped the potential of technology to radically impact teaching and learning.

THE PRINCIPAL AS TECHNOLOGY LEADER

Clearly, leadership plays a key role in successful reform. Knezek (2001), director of the Technology Standards for School Administrators project, recently stated,

> Integrating technology throughout a school system is, in itself, significant systemic reform. We have a wealth of evidence attesting to the importance of leadership in implementing and sustaining systemic reform in schools. It is critical, therefore, that we attend seriously to leadership for technology in schools. (p. 5)

Today's rapidly changing environment requires the principal as technology leader to become involved in discovering, evaluating, installing, and operating new technologies of all kinds, while keeping teaching and student learning as the guide and driving force behind it all. Vaill (1998) issues an accompanying caution: "The technologies the organization employs entail learning time to exploit their productive and economic potential" (p. 45). If schools are constantly "upgrading" their technologies, they may never reach a productive flow of instruction, a flow on which effective teaching and student learning are based.

Lou Gerstner (1994), CEO of IBM, believes that nothing matters more to America's schools than finding competent principals to lead them. Looking closely at principal preparation programs at our universities, the role of the principal as *technology* leader is only mentioned *in passing*. The topic is generally mentioned in a course such as "The Principalship," but for the most part, such a discussion highlights the principal's need to use technology for personal management skills. Budgets are prepared on spreadsheets, parent letters require a word processor, and occasionally the principal must use a database for compiling certain kinds of *administrivia*. Rarely, though, are principals-in-training provided any education related to the importance of creating a school environment conducive to maximizing the use of technology in the curriculum. Is it really surprising, then, to find many school technology programs led by *significant others*, rather than the principal?

Few would deny that the decision-making process regarding technology is shouldered by the building principal. Here are two areas in which the principal can help change the focus and begin effectively implementing technology in our schools.

1. It's not really about the boxes and wires. It's about what we do across those boxes and wires and with the boxes and wires, so that we enhance and enrich the human intelligence that we have (Lemke, 1998).

2. Equally important is the focus on conceptual knowledge of how technologies can be used to augment student learning (Creighton, 1999).

THE PROBLEM

We must be careful of defining technology implementation simply as the addition of hardware and software to our school environments. The principal's responsibility includes determining how much thought schools put into the role technology plays in teaching and student learning. Many schools have state-of-the-art hardware, computer labs, and other technology peripherals, but are using them in ways that will do little to enhance student learning in rigorous and challenging ways.

During my time as a school administrator in Idaho in the late '90s, the J. A. Albertson Foundation provided millions of dollars to school districts in the state. Much of the money, in the form of noncompetitive grants, funded two somewhat recognized early reading programs. Packaged with the programs were elaborate, expensive computer hardware and software. Schools across the state were "invited to the dance" and lined up to receive their "free" programs and computer equipment. Little thought was given to the validity and reliability of the reading programs. Less thought was given to whether or not the programs related to local district student needs as opposed to the foundation's possible political agenda.

The point of this example relates to the importance of the principal as technology leader. Technology leadership means much more than simply purchasing and implementing programs "stuffed" with fancy hardware and software. To really influence reform in schools, the principal as technology leader must stay focused on the individual needs of local teachers and students, rather than race to adopt the "flavor of the month" program. Clearly, schools do not have a very good track record in sustaining significant change. Principals as technology leaders are in the position to make sound instructional decisions regarding technology and program implementation. It is my hope that the chapters to come will help answer the "how" associated with such a daunting task.

STANDARDS AND ACCOUNTABILITY: THE NEWS IS NOT ALL BAD

Standards! Standards! "I got standards, you got standards, all God's children got standards" (Hoyle, 2001). My colleague John Hoyle, a professor of education administration at Texas A&M University, has written many articles devoted to the importance of standards, and in jest, points to the almost daily reference to standards in the field of education. Standards are the topic of discussion in our daily newspapers, journals, and other media. What professional journal has been published lately without some lead article devoted to standards and accountability? As I write this, I am also waiting to hear from the Journal of School Leadership, regarding a submitted article entitled "Standards for School Leaders: OK, but Don't We Have the Cart Before the Horse?" My stance is that we need to focus on rigorous selection procedures for principal candidates in our administration preparation programs before we can hope to address program standards in a meaningful way. But that's another story and not particularly related to our present discussion here.

For the most part, this discussion on standards has focused on teaching and learning in the areas of math, language arts, science, and social studies, with little mention of *technology.* However, this has recently changed. The International Society for Technology in Education (ISTE) has developed two sets of technology standards: (a) the National Educational Technology Standards for Students (NETS-S) and (b) the National Educational Technology Standards for Teachers (NETS-T). I will address a more recent set of *technology standards for school administrators* in Chapter 10. The Mid-continent Regional Education Laboratory (McREL) has compiled the volume *Content Knowledge: A Compendium of Standards and Benchmarks* (Kendall & Marzano, 2001), consisting of national and state standards for K–12 educators. Not only are authentic and in-depth standards for technology included, but these technology standards are offered at four levels: (a) Grades K–2, (b) Grades 3–5, (c) Grades 6–8, and (d) Grades 9–12. Let's "birdwalk" a technology standard across the different grade levels to show how teachers in all grades can address the standard in their classroom instruction. We'll focus on Number 3 of the 6 technology standards.

McREL Standard 3: Understand the relationships among science, technology, society, and the individual. How might a Kindergarten teacher cover this standard? Remember, standards are not an attempt to tell teachers how to teach. The teacher creates the strategy to address the standard. For example, here is an accompanying benchmark for McREL's Standard 3: *Knows that new tools and ways of doing things affect all aspects of life, and may have positive or negative effects on other people.* It is not difficult to see how a kindergarten teacher might use the example of the invention of firearms as a form of technology that has had an extremely negative impact on other people. On the other hand, these same youngsters would fully realize the powerful impact, both positive and negative, the invention of the automobile has had on society.

Now, can you see how this same technology standard and benchmark might be addressed by teachers in Grades 3–5, 6–8, and 9–12? Herein lies the power of standards—they are not grade specific and therefore leave room for much creativity in teaching. And standards help in demonstrating how educators can address the same knowledge, skill, or disposition across all grade levels.

As technology leaders, you are encouraged to become more familiar with the McREL Compendium of Standards and Benchmarks in all the content areas. But, certainly, it is equally important to include the technology standards in your instructional leadership (see Resource B).

Standards and accountability for technology implementation must now be included in all of our instructional dialogue and planning. In addition to asking teachers to become technologically competent, we are also asking them to integrate technology in a way that increases students' learning in all subject areas, in addition to becoming technologically competent.

STANDARDS? YES, BUT BE CAREFUL

As we discuss and consider the use of standards, I suggest a caution. The reasons for this are quite important: (a) standards often divert attention and focus back toward hardware and software and basic skills and competencies, and (b) standards have a tendency to draw planners and organizers toward goals/objectives that are not pertinent to their unique/individual education settings. In addition, much research (Achilles, 2001; Coleman, 2001; English, 2000) posits that standards are not generally reliable and valid and are extremely difficult (or impossible) to measure. Those of us in education leadership preparation programs are well aware of the controversy concerning the Interstate School Leaders Licensure Consortium (ISLLC) and the National Council for Accreditation of Teacher Education (NCATE) standards. Some feel the standards movement is occurring from outside their field and being imposed from accrediting agencies. Still others question how we might actually measure such standards. This controversy has mellowed over the last few years, and is especially silent now with the recent directives from the president and state legislators to emphasize accountability. But to repeat the caution from above, principals as technology leaders must stay focused on aligning standards and benchmarks with the local and district curriculum.

So, what about standards for technology? Most well-known are the recent technology standards developed by the International Society for Technology and Education (ISTE). These standards admittedly focus on use of technology by teachers and students—certainly important for principals to be familiar with. But they all neglect one thing: the realization that school principals play the critical role of determining how well technology is used in our schools. There is better news: This author strongly recommends that all school leaders become familiar with, and utilize, the set of standards developed by the Technology Standards for School Administrators Collaborative (TSSA Collaborative, 2001). "These standards enable us to move from just acknowledging the importance of administrators to defining the specifics of what administrators need to know and be able to do in order to discharge their responsibility as leaders in the effective use of technology in our schools" (p. 1).

For more information on the Technology Standards for School Administrators Collaborative, visit www.iste.org, or for individual copies of the standards, email the North Central Regional Technology in Education Consortium: ncrtec@ncrel.org

TECHNOLOGY COUNTS 2001

Recent reports from *Education Week's* "Technology Counts 2001" issue highlight additional good news for school leaders. Though we have a long way to go, the following findings reveal a positive climate and suggest the time is right to address a more powerful impact and potential for technology to affect teaching and learning.

1. In 2001, 76% of teachers surveyed stated they use computers for planning and/or teaching; 63% reported they use the Internet for instruction; and 77% said they have email addresses.

2. Though many states have technology standards for teachers and principals, 35 states report they also have technology standards for students.

3. The ratio of students per instructional computer shows a U.S. average of 4.9, ranging from 3.0 in Wyoming to 6.5 in Rhode Island. In addition, 94% of the nation's schools report Internet access for students.

4. Ninety percent of the students surveyed said it was "always" or "usually" easy to find an available computer at school.

5. Sixty-eight percent of the students said their teachers assign homework that requires the use of a computer. Students reported that the three most popular activities they use school computers for are (a) to do research for school

assignments (96%), (b) to write papers (91%), and (c) to do homework (62%). (pp. 12 – 36)

SO, WE BETTER HURRY, HUH?

No, I don't think we need to hurry. As a matter of fact, I suggest that part of our present dilemma relates to our pressing desire *to be first, rather than the best*. First to get the latest in hardware and software; first to become connected to the Internet; first to get in line for state and federal technology grant monies; first to get on the standards bandwagon. On and on and on! In our haste, we sometimes skip the important step of asking whether or not all the latest technology fits with our institution's instructional goals and objectives.

This author confesses with some embarrassment that a few years ago, as district superintendent in a central California school district, an emphasis was placed on being first, rather than the best. As the school district planned for technology in the midst of building construction, architects advised that the future of net-working was going to be Fiber Distributed Data Interface (FDDI). Wanting to be first on the block with fiber, we decided on pulling strands of fiber through a conduit underground, through campus buildings, rooms, ceilings, broom closets, and so forth. Today, a decade later, miles of unused fiber gather dust under the ground and in building walls across the campus. Though fiber is used in many cases, faster Ethernet technologies provided schools with a cheaper and more feasible alternative. As I write this chapter, I am made aware of wireless technologies available to schools. The point of this example is to emphasize the danger of concentrating too much on being first rather than the best. In hindsight, I wonder if we diverted valuable time and effort away from the quality of instruction and teacher development in an effort to be first with the latest fiber optics.

GOOD NEWS, YES; BUT NOW THE BAD NEWS

According to the cliché, along with good news comes some bad news. As encouraged and optimistic as I am about the potential for technology to radically influence student learning (and teaching), I must admit my concern for some negative trends we observe in our schools and wonder whether we are doing enough as technology leaders.

As technology leaders, we need to become aware of the "bad news" and use this awareness and knowledge to build our technology plans for the future. Later in the book, I will discuss the importance of conducting needs assessments in preparation for effective strategic planning in technology. I argue that the real power and potential of technology to influence student learning lies within the "bad news" or our "deficiencies." For that reason, I want to devote the next chapter to looking closely at some of these deficiencies and talk about how we might address them in a constructive and positive way.

CHAPTER TWO

Are Schools and Technology Leaders Doing Enough?

Asking my readers to look beyond the machines (boxes and wires) for a moment, I want to focus on whether or not we still have a *digital divide* in our schools. In other words, though we seem to have adequate computers and Internet access in our schools, are we certain that all of our students—regular education and special education, low achievers and high achievers, girls and boys, white and minority, wealthy and poor—are included and receive equal access to and the same appropriate high level instruction with technology? As a base, I use the May 10, 2001, issue of *Education Week*, "Technology Counts 2001," for pertinent data to help understand the role technology plays in our schools.

I want to reiterate the importance of disregarding the number of machines present in our schools for the purpose of looking closely at what schools and school leaders are doing (or not doing) beyond the machines themselves. For example, many would argue that we have closed the gap between poor urban schools and wealthier suburban schools regarding the ratio of computers to students. Those who support such an argument point to the evidence that students in poorer schools have one computer for every 5.3 students—not far from the national average of one computer for every 4.9 students (*Education Week*, 2001).

Stay with me for a moment. If we desegregate the data a bit further, we begin to see a picture of inequity and disparity in how technology is actually implemented or used in our schools. Herbert Kohl, the director of the Center for Teaching Excellence and Social Justice at the University of San Francisco, upon visiting schools across the nation, reports that students and teachers in predominantly minority schools are more likely to use technology for minimal skills such as drill and practice and test-taking strategies. On the other hand, teachers and students in wealthier white schools are using technology for such things as creating Web sites and multimedia presentations.

To guide our look at technology use beyond the machines, we will focus on *Education Week*'s report of other variables: (a) limited-English speakers, (b) students in rural schools, (c) students living in poverty conditions, (d) minority students, (e) female students, and (f) low-achieving students. If number of machines and funding for technology are constant, what do we see happening to students in these different groups?

WEALTHY SCHOOLS
VERSUS POORER SCHOOLS

As reported earlier, wealthy and poor schools have similar amounts of hardware (e.g., 5.3 students per computer for poor schools compared with 4.9 students per computer in wealthy schools). Let's now consider what the U.S. Department of Education reports when comparing the difference in Internet access between wealthy and poor schools. Wealthy schools were defined as those with fewer than 11% of students qualifying for free/reduced-price lunches, and poorer schools were defined as those with 71% or more students qualifying for free/reduced-price lunches. From 1994 to 1999, wealthy schools increased their Internet access from 4% to 74%, while for the same period, poorer schools increased their Internet access from 2% to only 39% (*Education Week*, 2001).

So what might these data mean to us as technology leaders? Let me share an observation of mine here in the state of Texas. As you probably are aware, Texas (and some other states) currently equates the success of schools with their standardized test scores (Texas Assessment of Academic Skills), determining the school's performance as exemplary, recognized, acceptable, or low performing. Visiting low-performing schools and exemplary schools, one notices similar inventories of computer labs and individual computers in classrooms. What is different is how and how much the technology is used. For example, exemplary schools generally utilize technology more often and in more higher-level ways (e.g., Internet use, data collection and analysis, and research projects). In low-performing schools (generally), one often observes less usage of technology and when used, more lower-level uses (drill and practice and word processing) are common.

First of all, there is some evidence indicating a relationship between wealth and high performance and high poverty and low performance (National Center for Education Statistics, 2000). But I think something else is at play in my observation above. It is my contention (which I have no empirical data to support) that schools labeled as low performing or even acceptable do not place an especially high priority on technology. There is so much emphasis on and pressure to raise test scores that technology takes a back seat to more traditional instructional strategies; and if technology is used, the emphasis is more likely to be on drill and practice and test-taking skills. Exemplary schools, on the other hand, seem to place a higher priority on technology with frequent use of higher-level activities such as Internet use and Web page construction. My point is that I suspect the high emphasis on standardized testing results in this observed disparity between exemplary and low-performing schools.

Let me conclude the discussion about technology implementation in poor and wealthy schools with a report from the Maryland State Department of Education (Johnson, 2001). Though I'm not aware of the data from other states, I suspect the findings would be similar. In Maryland, the number of schools reporting that their students regularly use technology to gather information from such sources as the Internet decreases as the percentage of students receiving free and reduced-price lunches increases.

Maryland students at wealthier schools are more than twice as likely as their peers in poorer schools to use technology to gather, organize, and store information. They are also three times more likely to use technology to perform measurements and collect data.

GENDER AND TECHNOLOGY IMPLEMENTATION

We have suspected for some time that we may unintentionally favor boys over girls in the area of technology. Except for the occasional example to the contrary, my experience in public schools reveals that girls are often intimidated by the large number of males in technology-related classes.

In response to the gender issue, some researchers argue that the gender gap is perceived rather than real. For instance, Judith Kleinfeld from the University of Alaska, Fairbanks, states that the low number of females in technology-related courses only points to the process of female students choosing to pursue different interests (Gehring, 2001).

Again, reflecting back on my experience in K–12 education, guidance counselors and high school teachers often inadvertently steered female students away from science and technology options. Only a few years ago, a certain high school guidance counselor advised the daughter of this author away from a certain California university because it had a reputation for a strong curriculum in computer science. I am not suggesting that any discrimination against girls is intentional, and I'm not suggesting that curriculum directors, school counselors, or other school leaders set out to dissuade girls from the opportunities to explore technology-related courses. There are many societal reasons for such practices to occur.

I am suggesting, however, that the principal as technology leader must pursue continual and intentional efforts to make certain the doors are as wide open for female students as for male students. Let's take a look at some data reported in *Education Week's* report, "Technology Counts 2001."

Marcia Greenberger, a copresident of the National Women's Law Center, contends that schools have not kept pace with the business world in creating an equal opportunity environment (Gehring, 2001).

> Women and girls are not getting the education they need to prepare them for high-wage careers in areas such as computers and engineering. Even with all the advancements for women, many job-training and career programs are still segregated by sex, with female students in classes such as cosmetology and typing, that lead to traditionally female, low-wage careers. (p. 18)

I'm not sure the situation is improving. The College Board reports that of the approximately 20,000 students who took the Advanced Placement (AP) computer science exam in 2000, only 15% were girls. In addition, in 1998, women received 27% of the undergraduate degrees in computer science, actually down from 37% in 1984 (Gehring, 2001).

Earth-shattering? Perhaps not. Relevant to the role of principal as technology leader? I suggest so. Two points should be made, the second of which is most important.

1. The principal as technology leader must make certain that schools are an equal-opportunity environment, for both genders as well as for other special populations.

2. Not willing to concede that girls in general lack an interest in technology-related courses, let's assume for a moment that to be the case. An important role for the principal as technology leader is to integrate and infuse technology use throughout all subject areas such as history, language arts, music, and drama. It is the belief of this author that we as leaders must expand technology concepts and use beyond the traditional computer science course. Including technology in all content courses ensures that all interest areas are covered and narrows the gender gap.

LOW AND HIGH ACHIEVERS

Does the following scenario sound familiar? We see computers in classrooms too often used as a reward for high achievers: "As soon as you finish your work, you can work on the computer." That we see these same students playing games on the computer is another issue; but what opportunity for access do the low achievers have? In addition, we often see the computer used as a substitute for effective classroom management: Some teachers use the computer as a means to keep the class troublemaker occupied.

According to the 1998 *Teaching, Learning, and Computing* document by the Center for Research on Information Technology and Organizations at the University of California, Irvine, "teachers of low-achieving classes use substantially more skills-based software, while teachers of advanced students use a mix of more sophisticated programs" (*Education Week*, 2001, p. 22). In addition, studies conducted at the University of Pittsburgh revealed that low-performing students tended to have far less access to computers than high-achieving students (Kennedy Manzo, 2001).

Here again, the problem is not so much a lack of "boxes and wires" or access to them, but how the "boxes and wires" are used. Take for example the use of the Internet: Teachers tend to view the use of the Internet as a reward or privilege rather than a resource beneficial to all students. Especially with low-achieving students, many teachers view the computer as a remedial tool, used primarily for drill and practice of basic skills. Principals as technology leaders must help teachers move beyond the practice of using computers in such restricted and minimal ways. Until we begin to change mind-sets, attitudes, and beliefs about the potential of technology to positively and radically improve achievement for all groups of students, adding to our inventory of boxes and wires and software will have little impact.

MORE BAD NEWS

Research reveals evidence of other special populations getting the short end of the stick regarding access and quality of instruction with technology. Rural schools, though many have Internet connections, are often wired with less than state-of-the-art capacity lines. Though most larger urban schools are wired with fiber-optic cable lines, many rural schools' computers function with one single dial-up telephone line.

Students with special needs (physical and mental disabilities) continue to receive less than adequate attention around the use of technology. People with disabilities have encountered a number of barriers in technology, such as computer terminals inaccessible to wheelchairs and software that is incompatible with adaptive devices employed by the disabled to use computers and other technology (U.S. Department of Commerce, 1999).

Bilingual and English as a second language programs (ESL) that tend to be poorly supported and funded in the first place, and tend to be viewed as add-on programs, are less likely to receive computers than are regular mainstream classrooms. A more thorough investigation shows bilingual and ESL classrooms with the older machines and outdated drill and practice software.

CONCLUDING THOUGHTS

Needless to say, much evidence exists indicating schools are not doing enough to see that all students get the technological skills and abilities they will need in the future. In addition, much emphasis in the area of technology is still focused on the computer as a remedial tool to reinforce basic skills. We are also found guilty of excluding certain special groups from the rich experiences we provide for regular and high-achieving students.

A growing body of research shows that teachers tend to integrate technology into lessons much less with low-achieving students than with high achievers (*Education Week*, 2001). Teachers of bilingual students also limit the uses of technology in their classes. Granted, we pressure teachers to focus their work with special-needs students on basic and remedial skills: and many teachers say they must forego technology use to cover all of the prescribed curriculum, especially with students who possess weaker skills. Here's an important question for the principal as technology leader to begin to address: Why do we seem to associate technology use more with high-achieving students and less with low-achieving students?

And so we come to the grand paradox for the principal as technology leader to consider: The potential for technology presents both the greatest opportunity and the greatest threat to schools and their leaders. If we continue on the same path, we run the risk not only of wasting a lot of time and money in the process but negatively affecting the minds and lives of students. On the other hand, if we insist on using technology to improve achievement and opportunities for all students, a brighter horizon is in sight.

CHAPTER THREE

Why Do Technology Programs Fail?

Working with school districts in Wyoming, Idaho, California, and Texas, and serving as director of the Administrative Technology Center in the Intermountain Region, I have worked with many innovative teachers and administrators and been involved with the implementation of many technology programs. Also, having worked in four university principal preparation programs, I have observed numerous technology programs in schools, both successful and unsuccessful. Over the years, my colleagues and I have wrestled with what really makes an effective technology program, and as important, what reasons cause many technology efforts to fail in our schools. My particular expertise in this area includes many "scars" received from having many of my own technology programs as a school administrator fail to have a significant impact on teaching and learning. To be perfectly honest, I suspect I have had more experience with failed efforts than successful ones.

So first of all, I hope you agree with me that people (including principals as technology leaders) learn a great deal from failed efforts, as long as they immediately make adjustments and corrections in the program. We all are aware of those administrators who throw in the towel at the first sign of less-than-desired results, but with the fast-paced change we face with the implementation of technology, it is important for us to learn from the mistakes and stay on track. The one consistent characteristic of effective principals as technology leaders is their ability to take two steps forward for every unexpected step backward. Someone once said that the real definition of an effective leader is the ability to get up just one more time than the number of times he or she falls down.

Let me share some recent studies in leadership related to principals and superintendents. I think a connection can be made to our discussion of technology implementation in our schools. For decades, those in the field of education leadership have studied the characteristics and constructs of effective leadership. Along with the research on leadership done in the business world, library and bookstore shelves are crowded with books and manuals on the subject. We've determined that leaders need to be competent at such things as planning, organizing, problem solving, vision building, communication, and instructional supervision, among others (I address some of these constructs in a later chapter when discussing the evaluation of faculty's use of technology in the classroom). But not until the research by Davis (1998) did we really begin to understand what is necessary to effectively lead schools. Davis took a fresh and innovative step by moving beyond *effective* characteristics of leadership and looking more specifically at what causes *ineffective* leadership. In other words, why do certain principals and superintendents lose their jobs or get demoted to lesser administrative roles? What traits and characteristics (good or bad) contribute to ineffective leadership? My point is that when we addressed what *ineffective* leadership looked like, we began to get a clearer picture and better understanding of characteristics of *effective* leadership. I suggest we use the same strategy to identify characteristics of effective technology programs: Why do some technology programs fail?

In my work with school district administrators and teachers as well as aspiring principals at the university, I began to identify some common themes as to why programs were failing. Over the years, I compiled these responses from my classes and visits to schools. Over 500 principals, superintendents, board members, teachers, and other technology leaders contributed their feedback to my question: Why do technology programs fail? I would like to share the results of my informal, not so empirical study with you.

Though many different responses surfaced, the three most frequently given were the following:

1. Inappropriate leadership—too little or too much

2. Moving too fast, without sufficient and supportive staff development

3. Failure to get the right people on board

LACK OF APPROPRIATE LEADERSHIP

It may not surprise you that my somewhat self-selected sample listed a lack of leadership as a factor for failing technology programs. But please notice my inclusion of the word *appropriate* in this section heading. Looking closely at the responses indicating a lack of leadership, I discovered that they fell into two subgroups, best described with the following quotes:

> "The principal came here two years ago with an agenda to implement *his* technology program. We had no say or input— 'just do it my way.'"

> "The principal was nowhere to be found when we were dealing with technology. She hired an outside consultant (retired navy captain) with no education experience, just a knowledge of the machines and wiring."

Think for just a moment about the existing technology plan (if you have one) in your school. Many have been designed by a technology coordinator (or some such title) with little input from other members of the school community. Please understand, I am not downplaying the importance of such folks in our districts: They are necessary for the effective implementation of technology to improve teaching and learning. But the result is often that the coordinator takes on the responsibility of leadership in technology, assuming a "mantle of techno-mysticism" (Ringle & Updegrove, 1998, p. 3), and exercising near-total control over the planning process.

A second scenario, equally present in our schools, reveals the school leader as little more than an office clerk to the technology planning process, assigning disinterested and disconnected committees to make the necessary decisions related to the implementation of technology. This situation is likely more dangerous and counterproductive than the first.

Effective leadership for technology planning must involve the principal as instructional leader supporting and driving the process forward, identifying issues for decision making, then seeking input and involvement from teachers and other stakeholder groups. The principal must guard against an individual (including him- or herself) fostering a personal agenda at the expense of focusing on the needs of the entire school community.

My point is that school technology programs can suffer as severely from too much leadership as they can from too little—hence my emphasis on a lack of *appropriate* leadership.

Too Much Leadership

Perhaps you are familiar with the principal (or other individual) who assumes a role of pushing technology purchase and implementation as a personal agenda and maintains total control over the entire process. The planning committee (if there is one) is chaired by the principal; the budget is controlled by the principal, resulting in hardware and software showing up in some classrooms and not others; and technology reports are issued monthly to the board of trustees by guess who—the principal.

When talking in-depth with this kind of technology leader, we often hear the response that the purchase and implementation of technology is a "no brainer." Why, they ask, is there any question that we must move quickly in this direction?

The appropriate style of leadership for technology implementation is no different from leadership in general: The first step must involve input from all stakeholders. Before implementing any technology in the school, the principal as technology leader must bring all faculty and staff (and representatives of the community) into the process. What other new strategy or program has ever succeeded without involvement and commitment from all involved?

Too Little Leadership

In my visits to school districts, I am equally alarmed to see situations where the school principal is not a player in the technology program at all. In many cases, school administrators have hired outside consultants or technology experts who are not familiar with curriculum and instruction. In addition, such a consultant is not a member of the education community and is often not accepted by faculty and staff as one who understands the classroom environment.

In order for the implementation of technology to be successful and effective, schools must be careful about external management or leadership. Yes, we sometimes need the help of experts from outside our immediate school environment, but often those experts are not familiar with the special needs of our school and/or district, therefore offering advice and council not particularly helpful to our needs. Some would say (this author included) that in this case, the school principal is really neglecting his or her responsibility to manage technology in such a way as to meet institutional goals and objectives.

One might reasonably ask, how can the principal be the technology leader if he or she is not technologically competent or knowledgeable? I am not suggesting that principals must avoid the use of technological experts from outside the school environment. The value of outside expertise and experience is not in question here. The core issue is this: The principal as technology leader must remain visible and involved in guiding the process of implementing technology, with teaching and learning as the driving force.

MOVING FORWARD WITHOUT SUFFICIENT AND SUPPORTIVE STAFF DEVELOPMENT

This heading presents another familiar theme, I suspect. Nothing new to those of you who've experienced implementing any new program or teaching strategy. Let me first state that the issue of staff development is so important that I address the topic in greater detail in Chapter 5. Allow me to reflect again on my observations of technology programs and discussions with teachers and administrators. The weaknesses in many staff development programs for teachers in our schools are many, but here again some common themes appear.

1. Much training but little education

2. Little ongoing support for newly acquired skills and ideas

Much Training But Little Education

Rebore (1998) and Robbins (1982) remind us that adult learning consists of two processes: (a) training and (b) education. *Training* is defined as the process of learning a set of skills that are programmed behaviors. This involves providing teachers with skills to better perform their jobs. *Education*, on the other hand, involves understanding and interpreting information, rather than just learning to use word processing, spreadsheets, and databases. Don't get me wrong—these are important skills for teachers. But if staff development focuses only on the acquisition of basic skills to the exclusion of understanding the teaching/learning process, we are missing the opportunity to implement technology in meaningful ways.

My observations reveal excessive use of training in our schools regarding technology. We spend our staff development time, which is minimal at best, focusing on training teachers to use technology to write letters to parents, input grades, write discipline referrals, and keep attendance. Certainly in today's computerized society, these skills are important. But very little of staff development that I observed in our schools facilitates the understanding of the teaching/learning process related to technology or helps teachers create the educational environment that uses technology to positively affect student learning.

To paraphrase the words of a former dean, you train animals, but teachers on the other hand are developed and educated. Because technology in our schools naturally involves such obvious skills, I contend we have a tendency not to look further.

Little Ongoing Support

From the research quoted in Chapter 2, *Education Week's* "Technology Counts 2001," we find that 43% of teachers surveyed site the lack of administrative support as a barrier to using computers and the Internet in classroom instruction. This is not a particularly encouraging finding. However, keeping with the theme of this book, I think much more can be learned by focusing on weaknesses rather than strengths. Principals as technology leaders and university preparation programs must address this pressing issue of lack of administrative support for technology programs.

Rebore (1998) describes the necessary steps to establishing program support. Though addressing general education, I think his model is very appropriate to technology leaders.

Step 1. The school board must set the stage by creating a positive climate for the program and provide the necessary funding and policies for implementation.

Step 2. The central office administration is responsible for creating a plan for management and supervision of the program.

Step 3. Building principals are responsible for identifying the knowledge, skills, and abilities that are needed to carry out the goals and objectives of the program.

Step 4. Teachers and staff must be included in program planning if they are expected to commit to implementation of the program.

Good quality administrative support usually starts with staff development programs for teachers. Again, we will look at this issue in greater detail in a later chapter. A recent poll of our nation's schools related to the role of staff development for technology implementation draws additional attention to the lack of support as a characteristic of ineffective technology programs.

In a 2001 poll of 50 states, *Education Week* found that states' requirements for technology-related professional development are dismal to say the least. Of the 20 states that specifically require schools or districts to set aside time for professional development for teachers, only 4 (Arkansas, Florida, Tennessee, and West Virginia) have such a requirement for technology-related professional development. This finding implies that the majority of states fail to value the connection between the appropriate use of technology and providing time and resources supporting related staff development. A critical need exists for principals at the local level to have ongoing dialogue with faculty, boards of education, and community members, highlighting the importance of professional development for teachers.

CONCLUDING THOUGHTS

It is the author's opinion that perhaps schools implement technology too quickly rather than gradually connecting technology to all aspects of the school culture and curriculum. Schlechty (1997) contributes insightfully to the discussion of radical change versus gradual change.

When technology implementation takes place gradually, those who are most affected (teachers and students) "have some choice as to when, how, and whether they will participate in and adopt the new technology" (p. 27). If technology implementation is gradual or incremental, teachers and principals have time to adjust and modify their roles and their commitment to the new technology. This strategy seems to deliver less turmoil and disruption to the existing culture and structure of the school community. Even the individual who chooses not to participate at all is less threatened and is provided with more time to consider joining the implementation.

On the other hand, when technology is introduced more radically, "choice regarding the use of the new technology is limited" (Schlechty, 1997, p. 27). Teachers (and principals) feel more overwhelmed and disrupted by it all. We all know how people commonly react to too much change too quickly: They dig in their heels and refuse to move. But when technology implementation is more gradual and purposeful, teachers can grow more comfortable with the change and are allowed time and opportunity to have more choice and input.

The principal as technology leader must be careful and not be tempted to allow the "lightening speed" of the technology revolution to drive the bus. For too long, we have been guilty of adapting our schools (and our learners) to technology; we must now work at adapting technology to our learners.

CHAPTER FOUR

Strategic Planning for Technology

An Oxymoron?

A s early as 1993, Lumley warned, "A common thread running through American education is a lack of sys-tematic planning for technology, and this may be a major reason why schools are behind other segments of society in technology" (p. 6). I suspect some progress has been made since then, and we all have technology plans of some sort on our shelf. However, too many of our technology plans have better intentions than results. All too often, technology is implemented at the building and district level with the absence of a strategic plan addressing exactly how technology will become an integral part of teaching and learning.

We have a tendency to call just about anything a *technology plan.* Some are complex while others only shallowly cover specific programs or projects. Still others are "highly technical," created by a few and understood by fewer still. I admit that many of the technology plans developed in the districts I worked with in the late '80s and early '90s took their familiar positions on the shelf along with other school improvement plans.

Ringle and Updegrove (1998) queried more than 150 technology officers in higher education around the country. Though the study involved institutions of higher education, the results have significant implications for K-12 school leaders. Roughly 10% of the respondents indicated that they simply don't do strategic technology planning, saying it is a frustrating, time-consuming endeavor that distracts from rather than contributes to the real work of building and maintaining an effective technology program. The researchers further state the following:

> Getting bogged down in lengthy, complex, and confusing technology planning is one of the most expensive—and self-defeating—experiences an institution can undertake. However, the alternative—to simply fly by the seat of one's technological pants—is hardly a sensible option. (p. 5)

The goal of this chapter is to emphasize the components of effective planning for technology and to present a relatively simple approach to planning for the appropriate management of technology in educational settings. I suggest Cheryl Lemke, director of the Milken Exchange on Educational Technology, is correct in advising, "there should be no technology plan, there should be a school improvement plan that has technology as an important component in it" (Lemke, 1998, p. 8). Approaching from this perspective helps us to see that the important piece of strategic planning for technology implementation is the learning—it's not the boxes and wires.

SO, WHAT'S THE PROBLEM?

As with many other aspects of strategic planning, educators often spend enormous amounts of time and energy developing complex plans that have a short life of applicability but a long life on the shelf. Strategic planning does not have to be that complex or time-consuming. Simply put, effective planning identifies where to go, justifies why, and shows how we get there.

We must learn how to develop simple but effective technology plans that produce high-quality student outcomes with a minimum of faculty frustration and resistance. The author's intent is to present such a model here. Strategic planning for technology is not an oxymoron—the two must go hand-in-hand.

CREATING A STRATEGIC PLAN
FOR TECHNOLOGY: NOT SO FAST!

This is the step so many of us skip—deciding on where we want to go. The research of Ringle and Updegrove (1998) can help with this initial decision, especially when we look at their findings concerning reasons for technology planning failure. They identified four common responses regarding technology plan failure: (a) failure to tie technology to institutional mission and priorities, (b) failure to get the right people on board, (c) excessive focus on technical detail, and (d) lack of suitable leadership. Let's look at each.

Failure to Tie Technology to
Institutional Mission and Priorities

Recall Lemke's suggestion that we should not have technology plans but school improvement plans with technology as a component. I think she is addressing our failure to tie the technology plan to all other aspects of our operation. Our strategic plans must be linked to teaching, student achievement, staff development, parent involvement, teacher workloads, instructional delivery, and as much as it hurts me to say, even tied to our state and national testing programs. Too many technology plans view these issues as other programs with little relationship to where we want to go regarding technology implementation. Consequently, too often the technology plan is "orphaned" (Ringle & Updegrove, 1998, p. 3), designed and implemented independently of other institutional priorities. So how do we tie the plans together?

Failure to Get the Right People on Board

Ineffective technology plans (or many others) focus on change as something you do to people, rather than something you do with them. Each school district or building has people who can assist in moving technology plans forward and others who can (and may wish to) put a roadblock in front of the efforts. Principals and other school leaders must not be tempted to exclude such "saboteurs" and include only the "trailblazers" in the planning process (Schlechty, 1997, p. 218). In actuality, many of our saboteurs were once trailblazers but the leaders whom they once followed, failed to give them support. Members from both sides of the fence must be brought into the technology planning process or the plan will go no further than intentions and fail to encounter results.

This weakness surfaced so often in my observations of technology programs that I want to devote Chapter 6 to how the principal as technology leader can effectively include both those who need no encouragement and those who are likely to resist the implementation of technology.

Excessive Focus on Technical Detail

If a strategic technology plan is composed of excessive details and analyses, it is a candidate for a long shelf life—at best, it is a blueprint for micromanaging. Few of us in education leadership really understand the complex technical side of technology, and to overemphasize it risks diminishing the interest and involvement of teachers and principals—the very folks who must implement and sustain a technology plan. A good, workable, proactive technology plan can take as little as one day to complete. The secret is understanding that strategic technology planning is a continuous process and needs only a brief, 1- to 2-page technology plan, devoid of excessive detail and technical jargon.

OK, THE STRATEGIC PLANNING PROCESS!

Strategic planning is the process of identifying the direction in which an organization should head, why it should head there, and how to tell when it has arrived (Kaufman, Herman, & Watters, 1998). Kaufman's strategic planning model incorporates needs assessment as a tool for defining an organization's direction and developing criteria for knowing when it has achieved its goals and objectives. The questions generated are simply these:

1. Where are we headed?

2. Why do we want to go there?

3. How will we know when we have arrived?

To assist with developing a strategic technology plan, let's visit the SWOT analysis for a helpful model.

THE SWOT ANALYSIS

Roger Kaufmann, from Florida State University, is credited with developing the SWOT (strengths, weaknesses, opportunities, threats) analysis as an organizational brainstorming activity in which stakeholders identify internal and external issues affecting an organization. We find the model extremely useful in the development of strategic technology planning.

The model is different than most because an equal consideration is suggested for both internal and external factors. We have a habit in education of viewing our schools (and districts) as entities within the architectural structures of our buildings, or at best, the space between our physical boundaries. Rarely do we look externally to consider strengths, weaknesses, threats, and opportunities for our programs. Some professionals argue that the external environment is the most practical area from which to develop an understanding of our organization's context.

We often look internally at the strengths and weaknesses in our school district, but rarely do we evaluate opportunities and threats. Even less often do we look carefully at these variables both inside (internal) and outside (external) our organization. Here is the real value of the SWOT model—it encourages us to take both an internal *and* external view of our district and its technology needs. To recap, the SWOT analysis does the following:

1. Identifies those supports (strengths) that are available to help implement our technology plan

2. Identifies those weaknesses that should be corrected to achieve the goals of our plan

3. Identifies the opportunities that exist that have not previously been utilized

4. Discovers the threats to achieving our goals

Table 4.1   A Partial SWOT Matrix for Technology Planning at Westside High School

	Strengths	Weaknesses	Opportunities	Threats
Internal data	* 70% of teachers have passed state technology exam.	* Emphasis is placed on drill and practice activities in classrooms.	* Several high school seniors have expertise to maintain computer hardware (e.g., CISCO training).	* Local teachers' union takes strong position opposing technology implementation.
External data	* Local university offers professional development in technology for teachers via Internet and ITV.	* University preparation programs are not adequately preparing teachers in the area of technology.	* Retired naval officer in community has expertise in maintenance of infrastructure.	* Parents have perceptions that students use computers for games, etc.
Analysis	* Consider stipends for teachers in the 70% group to mentor those lacking in technology skills.			* Consider inviting union representatives and parents to informative meetings.

Table 4.1 displays a SWOT matrix with data that may exist in your school and should be analyzed as you develop your strategic technology plan.

USING THE SWOT ANALYSIS TO DEVELOP THE STRATEGIC TECHNOLOGY PLAN

Before we look at how we can use the SWOT analysis to create our technology plan, let's revisit the four components of the analysis.

Strengths are areas of support already existing in our schools and need to be taken advantage of if our technology plan is to be successful. Leaders must look outside (externally) as well as inside (internally) to assess existing strengths. For example, internally we find that 70% of our teachers passed the State Technology Competency Exam, and externally we find the local university offers staff development to local schools in the area of technology. Both strengths need to be utilized in productive and constructive ways.

Weaknesses are barriers a district (or school) needs to break down in order to successfully implement a technology plan. Our SWOT analysis reveals an internal weakness of too much emphasis on basic math skills (*drill and kill*) activities in the lab and classrooms. Externally, we discover a lack of appropriate preparation for teachers and administrators in the university preparation programs. Look closely at specific weaknesses—often there are others lying just beneath them!

Opportunities are potential strengths that we have neglected, for whatever reason, to take advantage of. Looking closely, we discover that several of our high school students have the expertise and ability to maintain computer hardware. Reaching externally, outside of the school, we also have technical expertise in the form of retirees from business we can utilize in our plan. Though opportunities exist in both the internal and external environment, those existing internally are often overlooked. School districts tend to depend on help from outside sources, such as county offices of education and consultants. We often fail to take a close look in our own backyard!

Threats are also barriers and must be eliminated; but at the very least, our technology plan must include strategies for reducing the negative effects of both internal and external threats. In our hypothetical case, the local teachers' union has taken a strong position opposing the implementation of technology in our district, feeling that the funding could better be used for salaries and benefits. External to the district, we also find resistance from many of the parent and community groups—their resistance stems from concern that students are participating in computer games and other noncurricular activities.

Let's use the three questions generated earlier as our framework for a strategic technology plan. As we discuss each question, we will reflect back on our data collected in the SWOT analysis.

I suggest you pull out the blank analysis form in Resource A and take some notes regarding your own school or district as we cover the next three sections.

WHERE ARE WE HEADED?

A Change in Thinking

For too long, educational leaders have fallen prey to the habit of implementing technology plans that are technology-driven rather than curriculum-driven. *The technology exists, we've got to have it!* Sound familiar? We must reverse our thinking as we begin to answer the question, where are we headed? It requires considerable reflection and perhaps debate as to whether, and under which conditions, technology will enhance the quality of teaching and learning. We seem to be confusing "technology as tools" with "instructional design." Instructional design incorporates technology with knowledge of teaching and learning, while "technology as tools" is just that—"boxes and wires," often with little regard for how it impacts teaching and learning. We may be guilty of adapting learners to technology instead of adapting technology to learners.

I agree that in many of our schools today, we witness what Callister and Dunne posited in 1992:

> Most uses of technology are still based on the oldest learning theory of all: the master-apprentice, one-on-one tutorial, with monitor substituted for teacher as the tutor. Teachers no longer teach; instead, they are managers of relatively rigid delivery systems and immutable instructional content. While students sit at their workstations, vessels to be filled with facts suitably stored in machine-retrievable code, teachers oversee the operation like foremen in an automated factory. (p. 35)

Are We Really Using Technology to Improve Student Learning for All?

As much as we hate to admit it, evidence reveals much inconsistency in how we use technology to address the needs of both affluent and poor students, both minority and white students, both girls and boys, and both low-achieving and high-achieving students. These findings certainly suggest a lack of appropriate planning for technology as a curriculum-driven force. *These issues must enter the dialogue as education leaders think about effective planning for technology in our schools.* Here are some recent findings related to how we use technology in our schools, as reported in the May 2001 special edition of *Education Week*, entitled "Looking Beneath the Numbers to Reveal Digital Inequities."

1. In schools where reduced-price lunch rates are 11% or lower, 75% of classrooms have Internet access.

2. In schools where the free and reduced rate is 71% or more, only 39% of classrooms are connected to the Internet.

3. Students taking the Advanced Placement exam in computer science in the year 2000 consisted of 85% boys and 15% girls.

4. Teachers tend to integrate technology into instruction much less for low-achieving students than they do for high-achieving students.

5. Teachers of bilingual students are less likely to expose their students to technology in their classrooms or computer labs than teachers of fluent English-speaking students.

6. Students in schools in wealthier areas are more than twice as likely as their peers in poorer communities to use technology to gather, organize, and store data. They are three times more likely to use technology to perform measurements and collect data.

7. Though research reveals an overall use of lower-level activities in many schools, the general application of technology with low-achieving students is for "drill-and-practice" in academic skills.

8. The promise of equity of access between rural and urban schools is not yet realized. Cable modem service is available to less than 1% of towns with populations of fewer than 2,500 people.

9. Nearly half (24) states have no technology requirements in place for teachers in training prior to state licensure.

Pepi and Scheurman (1996) make a strong statement regarding the state of technology use in schools:

> Our observations of technology in the classroom reveal teachers most frequently using computers as a tool for drill and practice. Or worse, like television in the hands of many lazy instructors, it is used as an instrument of classroom management. Students often wile hours away on the Superhighway, and while there may be a good deal of incidental learning taking place, such activity is often justified in terms of "keeping them on task" rather than because there is evidence that it aides in the construction of meaningful knowledge. (p. 7)

So, Where *Do* We Want to Head?

The intent of this previous section is not to discourage or even criticize the deficiencies and weaknesses of technology implementation we find in many of our schools. It is to suggest that those responsible for planning technology implementation have failed to consider all of the existing factors that may or may not help with successful implementation of technology programs in our schools. When initiating the planning process, for example, how can we justify using district funds for programs that focus on one group (high achievers) and exclude another (low achievers)? How can we as educational leaders explain the failure of programs to give equitable opportunities to limited-English-speaking students or equal access to those of a particular gender?

I hope this illuminates why I was so hesitant to jump right in and create a strategic plan for technology implementation. We have lots of serious thinking to do first. And once we as school leaders have a handle on *where we want to head*, we begin the timely but crucial dialogue with our teachers, parents, students, and community members in an effort to involve all stakeholders in the planning process.

Let me assume that my readers generally agree with the findings presented above from *Education Week*, and that we are uncomfortable with the environment of technology implementation the research reveals. As we consider *where we want to head*, I think we can say with some certainty that we do *not* want to continue heading in the present direction. Therefore, we must *envision* another environment. As trite as it may sound, we are really looking for an *ideal vision* of technology implementation that we as a school or district can believe in and commit to.

Though this process must be your own and represent the beliefs and commitments of your school community, allow me to demonstrate my own thinking along this line. You may want to retrieve your SWOT analysis form from Resource A to follow along with the discussion that follows.

Let's reflect back on the Westside School District SWOT analysis and use that information to develop the first step in strategic planning, deciding "where we want to head." You may respond to some of my comments with, "But how can we do that? Where will the resources come from to implement that idea?" Remember, our goal here is to create the ideal vision—dealing with the how and why will come in Step 2 (Why do we want to go there?) and Step 3 (How will we know when we arrive?).

Continuing with our hypothetical model, our planning committee decides, after looking closely at the SWOT analysis and reflecting on some of the research, that we want the school to head in the following direction:

1. The Westside School District will decrease, and eventually eliminate, the use of classroom and lab activities fostering lower-level thinking skills such as drill and practice, games, worksheets, etc.

2. The Westside School District will strive to give equal access to technology (hardware, software, and support) to lower-achieving students and higher-achieving students (e.g., same level of technical support for general math classes and advanced calculus classes).

3. The Westside School District will contact the local university and set up a professional development program in technology for teachers and administrators.

4. The Westside School District planning committee, along with the building principal, will meet with the teachers' union leaders to begin a dialogue focusing on the importance of a strategic plan for technology. In addition, the building

budget will be discussed and attention drawn to the fact that salaries and benefits generally come from different revenue sources than supplies, equipment, and instructional materials involved in technology implementation.

5. The Westside School District planning committee will present a proposal to the Board of Education, suggesting the implementation of professional development activities, compensating teachers with technology expertise who mentor teachers in need of assistance.

The 5 directions listed above, and their development through the use of the SWOT analysis, demonstrate the simplicity of Step 1 in the planning process, as well as the importance of looking at both internal and external factors. Now that we have an idea of *where we want to head,* we will move on to *why we want to go there.*

WHY DO WE WANT TO GO THERE?

This step is not so easy, and is often neglected in the planning of any of our instructional programs or strategies. Educators are quick to decide where they want to go, but seldom give serious attention or consideration to why.

We have heard since 1983 (*Nation at Risk*) about the need to reform our public schools. Almost weekly, we read reports that educators are not keeping pace with the real world, and business leaders remind us we are not producing enough qualified workers. Other educators strongly cry out for education reform (Barth, 1990; Glickman, 1998; Goodlad, 1997; Schlechty, 1997; Sarason, 1997; Sergiovani, 1996).

Recently, researchers point out that technology may be of great help. Cuban (2001) believes instructional technology has unrealized potential for education reform. Schlechty (1997) states that there exists a "technological imperative," and that the "hope of American democracy and the economy resides in understanding the uses and misuses of technology" (p. 40).

We are being asked to do something never contemplated before: to provide a high-quality education to ALL students, not just an elite group of college prep students. A few decades ago, college prep meant a mere 10% of our students (Fullan, 2001). We must now prepare a large majority of students for college and provide an equally high quality education to all others.

Technology may be the vehicle to accomplish the daunting task before us. Why do we want to go there? Some would argue we have no choice. I disagree—we have a choice. Either we continue with business as usual or we take advantage of the potential of technology to help us with society's new expectation of us: that we educate all students to the same high degree.

HOW WILL WE KNOW WHEN WE GET THERE?

The SWOT analysis helped us identify specific technological needs of our school and helped with the decision of how we would address those needs. In the process, as we examined both external and internal data, we were able to analyze and implement a plan.

Crucial to determining how we will "know when we get there" is the creation and use of measurable performance targets or objectives. Ongoing evaluation and an emphasis on continuous improvement are also critical.

As an example, recall that the SWOT analysis identified an internal strength of 70% of our teachers passing the State Technology Competency Exam. Let's set a measurable performance target to insure continuous improvement. Table 4.2 displays data collected over the last four years, and we see the improvement up to the current year of 70%. However, our goal is to have all teachers competent in technology, so we have some ground to cover. Only through a regular and continuous monitoring of the program toward a measurable performance goal—100% competency—will we know when we have arrived.

Complex and complicated? Not really. Setting measurable performance targets provides the principal as technology leader with justifiable directions and targets and measurable criteria for success. Without such regular monitoring, we run the risk of making decisions based on intuition or "shooting from the hip." Strategic planning, along with measurable performance goals, allows the principal as technology leader to test the viability of

Table 4.2   Setting Performance Goals

	1997/98	1998/99	1999/00	2000/01	Performance Goal
Internal strength: 70% of teachers have passed state technology exam	20%	25%	50%	70%	100%

interventions and justify decisions made regarding the implementation of technology.

CONCLUDING THOUGHTS

Strategic planning for technology is not an oxymoron. It is crucial and necessary in order for school leaders to implement technology effectively. Strategic planning for technology, as stated earlier, is the process of identifying the direction our school should head, determining why it should go in that direction, and finally, deciding how we will know when we actually get there. During the process, the principal as technology leader must be certain that everything in the school (e.g., curriculum, staff development, etc.) aligns with technology implementation.

Identifying what direction we want to head should be based on our organization's needs and desires and focused on using our available resources—both financial and human; determining why we should head in that direction should be based on sound educational research; and determining how we will know when we get there requires the establishment of measurable goals and a continuous evaluation plan.

I cannot overemphasize the importance of keeping strategic plans for technology simple and understandable by all (both educators and noneducators). My past experience of evaluating technology programs for state departments of education revealed many long, detailed, complicated plans sitting on shelves beside other dusty documents.

I equally stress that the principal as technology leader should strive to integrate the technology plan into the school culture as much as possible. If technology is appropriately implemented, it is *woven into the fabric* of your school community and exists in harmony with all other aspects of your organization. Technology plans too separate and distant from institutional goals and objectives make it difficult to identify the connection between technology and the teaching and learning goals it is designed to support.

CHAPTER FIVE

Setting the Stage for Staff Development

Uniting Technology and Constructivist Teaching and Learning Environments

Staff development practices have undergone considerable change over the last two decades. Three trends contributing to the change are (a) results-driven education, (b) the systems approach to school organization, and (c) the emphasis on *constructivism* on teaching and learning (Rebore, 1998). All three have powerful implications for how we design and implement professional development programs for technology.

RESULTS-DRIVEN EDUCATION

Results-driven education has required us to change the behaviors and/or attitudes of teachers and staff. Even in our own administrative language, we talk about the need for effective administrators to possess not only certain knowledge and skills, but also particular dispositions or beliefs. How does this connect or relate to programs of professional development in technology? Our staff development efforts must address changing the way people think or what they believe about technology. We must move beyond the belief that technology's function is merely word processing or to serve as an electronic blackboard. Attempts to change teachers' beliefs or thinking about something are not only difficult, but often make *resisters* more resistant and *saboteurs* more likely to participate in sabotage activities.

THE SYSTEMS APPROACH

Thanks to the research of such folks as Peter Senge (1996), we've begun to engage in systemic thinking and planning and concerning ourselves with the interrelatedness of all aspects of our school or district. Thus, an innovative technological development such as the Internet has ramifications for the science department as well as the language arts program. Obviously, such a development also has ramifications for the home and other parts of the community. Again, does the systems approach to education administration have a relationship to technology staff development? I suspect we all agree that part of the essence of a systems approach is its interconnectedness across the entire organization (i.e., school district). Continue this thinking as we look at how technology should blend in with all aspects of our teaching, learning, staff development, community relations, and so forth. This draws attention to the importance of including *all* members of our school community in the process.

CONSTRUCTIVIST
TEACHING AND LEARNING

The third trend affecting staff development in education is likely the most significant and the one we need to address the most in our planning of staff development programs for technology. Constructivism presents the notion that learners (young and old) build knowledge structures in their minds rather than have the knowledge implanted by the teacher.

What does that mean in plain English? Constructivists view education less as a process in which the teacher educates the student and more as an active process of construction by the student.

Jacqueline Grennon Brooks (Brooks & Brooks, 1993) helps us understand the real meaning of constructivist teaching as she talks about reinventing the wheel:

> Although constructivism as a guiding principle in education is receiving more attention today than in the past, much confusion persists over its message and its implications. Suppes (1989), a critic of what he calls the romanticism of this approach, asks, "What are you going to do, reinvent the wheel?" (p. 909). The answer is "yes." In the ideal educational setting, students will reinvent the wheel, reinvent long division, rediscover horrors of war, and reinvent government. (p. 71)

Constructivists believe students are active seekers and constructors of knowledge—and students bring their own individual goals and curiosities to the classroom (Brooks & Brooks, 1993; Fosnot, 1993; Piaget, 1969). Thus, traditional teacher-centered instruction of predetermined plans, skills, and content is inappropriate (Brooks & Brooks, 1993, as cited in Nicaise & Barnes, 1996).

Another ingredient of constructivist teaching involves the opportunity of students to have social discourse and interaction. A discussion of constructivism would not be complete without reference to Vygotsky (1962), the now-famous learning theorist who suggested that cognitive development depends on the student's social interaction with others, where language plays a central role in learning. So, focusing on these ideas, the teacher's responsibilities involve creating classroom environments where students think, explore, and construct meaning, while including opportunities for students to have social interaction.

SO, WHAT DOES ALL THIS HAVE TO DO WITH TECHNOLOGY LEADERSHIP AND EFFECTIVE FACULTY DEVELOPMENT PROGRAMS?

First of all, we have reason to suspect that many of our classrooms today still focus on the more traditional practice of teachers disseminating knowledge with the expectation of students *magically* absorbing that knowledge and then regurgitating it back to us in some form of standardized test. Two questions must concern the principal as technology leader: (a) How prevalent are constructivist learning strategies in our classrooms presently? and (b) How can technology be used as a tool to support and encourage constructivist principles of learning?

We must visit the present dialogue in this regard. As constructivism has furthered our understanding of learning theory, many educators (including this author) believe computer technology can be used to continue and further enhance effective teaching and learning in today's classrooms. Others (Pepi & Scheurman, 1996) present a convincing argument, stating that "electronic technologies often are not used in ways consistent with constructivist principles of learning, and no reason exists to believe they will be in the near future" (p. 231). Honestly, my experiences show support for the first part of their statement—technologies are not often used in constructivist ways. What is exciting and encouraging, however, is that technologies have the potential for such support, and with appropriate instructional leadership by principals, technology can be an effective catalyst for educational reform.

THE ALL-TOO-OFTEN-OCCURRING PRACTICE

Let's take a look at how technology is being used in many of our classrooms. Remember one of our earlier questions—How prevalent are constructivist learning strategies in our classrooms presently?

Rather than reporting on my observations of classrooms in several states, let's address this question by setting forth a few key concepts of constructivism. As you read through them, ask yourself whether or not the use of technology in the classrooms you have witnessed takes any of these concepts into consideration.

Concept 1. The teacher must first help students build a foundation of skills and knowledge, but simultaneously allow and encourage students to use their creative abilities to solve real-world problems.

Concept 2. Students and teachers collaboratively negotiate both the means of instructional strategies and the content of the course.

Concept 3. Teachers approach instruction with two or three main ideas, rather than a long list of skills and objectives to be covered. And those few ideas are "explored" rather than "covered."

Concept 4. Social discourse—social interaction with others—plays a central role.

Concept 5. The role of the teacher changes from information provider and test creator to guide and problem and task presenter.

Unless your experience and observations are different from mine, I suggest that the current use of technology in the classroom takes few, if any, of these concepts into consideration. Instead, we see excessive use of drill and practice, absence of student interaction, and the lack of real-life problem-solving activities. In more cases than not, the student at the computer is so far away and disconnected from the teacher that the two could well be in different rooms.

A CAUTION TO THE
PRINCIPAL AS TECHNOLOGY LEADER

Although our understanding of learning has changed dramatically, the role of the computer in learning has pretty much remained the same—as a tutorial aid, mostly facilitating drill and practice activities. Herein lies the caution! Research seems to indicate that "technology has not radically changed the way we teach; instead, most technology mirrors traditional instructional pedagogy" (Nicaise & Barnes, 1996, p. 205). "Most uses of technology are still based on the oldest learning theory of all, the master-apprentice, one-on-one tutorial, with monitor substituting for teacher as the tutor" (Callister & Dunne, 1992, as cited in Pepi & Scheurman, 1996, p. 231). Critically looking at our appetite for computer technology, Pepi and Scheurman issue this warning:

As much reason exists to believe that computer technology will reinforce and maintain the traditional role of the teacher as to believe it will become the agent of positive institutional reform. An inherent danger in accepting technology as the catalyst for educational restructuring is that such a view enables us to ignore a more fundamental problem facing our schools, namely bad teaching. (p. 231)

IMPLICATIONS FOR TECHNOLOGY LEADER AND STAFF DEVELOPMENT

A major role for the principal as instructional leader (and technology leader) is to provide appropriate staff development programs that allow teachers to enhance skills and remedy deficiencies (Rebore, 1998, p. 163). As the principal evaluates and supervises teachers, staff development programs are essentially the vehicle for effective instructional use of technology. The all-too-common practice of "let's have a workshop" continues to make a bad situation worse. Workshops often are focused on one topic and not necessarily aligned with school objectives and goals. It's unreasonable to expect teachers to implement skills and knowledge acquired in a one- or two-hour workshop without opportunities for practice, feedback, and additional emphasis of those skills and knowledge.

Before we proceed with creating technology staff development programs, we must first agree about the importance of support and supervision during the implementation of new programs. Educators (Glatthorn, 1995; Rebore, 1998) point to the fact that a major reason why teachers perceive professional development activities as ineffective is because they receive little support for implementing newly acquired skills and ideas, and a lack of supervision during implementation.

CAN TECHNOLOGY SUPPORT AND ENCOURAGE CONSTRUCTIVIST PRACTICES?

Considering our second question, first recall the basic principles of constructivist teaching and learning. Let's begin to bring technology into the picture as we consider effective teacher development programs. Teachers can use technology to engage students in more meaningful learning than is presently occurring in many classrooms today. Technology can assist with conveying meaning to students in a social context, i.e., accompanied by interaction between the learner and other people. With careful planning of professional development programs, principals can successfully fulfill their significant and powerful role in improving teaching and learning.

To assist us in creating appropriate technology staff development programs for our schools, let's look at an Association for Supervision and Curriculum Development document entitled, *In Search of Understanding: The Case for Constructivist Classrooms.* Of particular interest is an article written by Grennon Brooks and Martin Brooks entitled "Becoming a Constructivist Teacher (1993)" which outlines 12 descriptors of constructivist teachers. These descriptors can serve as a framework for the design of effective technology staff development programs. Here are 3 of the 12 relevant descriptors from their research. Notice how I have tied each of them specifically to technology issues for demonstration purposes. The 9 descriptors that follow in the next section can be adapted to technology in similar ways.

Descriptor 1. Contructivist teachers encourage and accept student autonomy and initiative. Though we contend that students should be given the freedom and choice to explore concepts and information on their own and take responsibility for their own learning, much evidence exists that this is not truly the case in many classrooms regarding the use of technology. Too often, computer assignments consist of passive drill and practice activities with little opportunity for students to display autonomy and initiative.

Descriptor 2. Constructivist teachers use raw data and primary sources, along with manipulative, interactive, and physical materials. This descriptor focuses on the students using real-world data and other information to generate their own explanation and inferences about existing problems in our world. When teachers encourage students to wrestle with their own interpretation of existing phenomena, students must move beyond the usual mode of drill and practice, and be provided with opportunities to analyze, synthesize, and evaluate. Observing the common software used in many classrooms, one notices a lack of opportunity for students to experience multiple perspectives or critical thinking.

Descriptor 3. When framing tasks, constructivist teachers use cognitive terminology such as "classify," "analyze," "predict," and "create." Much of what transpires in today's classrooms involves multiple choice, such as asking students to select the correct answer from a list of options. Correct answers are provided quickly and too willingly by teachers. Observing what happens in the classroom regarding the use of technology reveals a similar practice. Students have little opportunity to predict or create their own interpretation of solutions to problems or endings to stories. Analyzing, interpreting, predicting, and synthesizing are mental activities that require students to make connections, delve deeply into texts and contexts, and create new understandings. (Brooks & Brooks, 1993)

THE REMAINING DESCRIPTORS OF CONSTRUCTIVIST TEACHERS

As you work with your plans for technology staff development, consider the other 9 descriptors of constructivist teachers set forth by Brooks and Brooks. Including these descriptors in your planning assures an emphasis away from traditional drill and practice activities and more toward an environment where students can use their creative, intellectual abilities to solve real-world problems. The remaining 9 descriptors are as follows:

Descriptor 4. Constructivist teachers allow student responses to drive lessons, shift instructional strategies, and alter content.

Descriptor 5. Constructivist teachers inquire about students' understandings of concepts before sharing their own understandings of those concepts.

Descriptor 6. Constructivist teachers encourage students to engage in dialogue, both with the teacher and with one another.

Descriptor 7. Constructivist teachers encourage student inquiry by asking thoughtful, open-ended questions and encouraging students to ask questions of each other.

Descriptor 8. Constructivist teachers seek elaboration of students' initial responses.

Descriptor 9. Constructivist teachers engage students in experiences that might engender contradictions to their initial hypotheses and then encourage discussion.

Descriptor 10. Constructivist teachers allow wait time after posing questions.

Descriptor 11. Constructivist teachers provide time for students to construct relationships and create metaphors. Encouraging the use of metaphor is another way to facilitate learning, bolstering their understanding of concepts.

Descriptor 12. Constructivist teachers nurture students' natural curiosity through frequent use of the learning cycle model, published by Adkins and Karplus in 1962 (cited in Brooks & Brooks, 1993). This model involves three steps: (a) teacher provides open-ended opportunity for students to question and interact with the material, (b) teacher introduces concepts aimed at focusing students' questions, and (c) teacher provides for concept application, which encourages students to work on new problems based on the concepts previously studied. The traditional teaching model avoids the discovery phase until last, with usually only the brighter students participating. Moving the discovery step up front allows for students of all abilities to experiment early on with ideas, hypotheses, and discovery. (Brooks & Brooks, 1993)

AN EXAMPLE OF STAFF DEVELOPMENT FOR TEACHERS IN TECHNOLOGY: LINKING TECHNOLOGY AND THE 12 DESCRIPTORS OF CONSTRUCTIVIST TEACHING

So how do we use technology to encourage students to exercise higher-order thinking skills? More important, how do we help teachers understand and value the connection? Allow me to present a staff development program used in a southeast Idaho school district, as they focused on using technology to encourage the components of constructivist teaching and learning. The following example is an actual staff development module used with K-8 teachers during the 2000-2001 school year.

The purpose of this professional development module was twofold: (a) to focus on the relationship between technology and constructivist learning principles and (b) to actually use technology as the medium for delivery of professional development to the district's teachers. The method of delivery was an asynchronous online course developed collaboratively by the building principal and a university professor in education leadership, who together monitored and guided the course delivery. The course, entitled *Uniting Technology and Constructivist Teaching and Learning Environments*, was offered to school faculty as a 3-credit master's level course. The principal's active participation was critical because it enabled her to acquire the same knowledge and understanding as the faculty.

The Internet platform used was Blackboard, a sophisticated software that encompasses course management, including (a) posting of assignments and readings, (b) discussion forums, (c) links to the World Wide Web for additional research and reading, and (d) an assessment component—all accessible any time of the day or night via an Internet connection. Teachers were able to enter the course from both school and home, affording a flexibility usually absent in professional development programs.

First Few Weeks

To develop a knowledge base of constructivist theory and principles, teachers read numerous articles posted in the course assignments area. Additional readings were assigned, detailing the Atkins and Karplus learning framework (Descriptor 12). The over-riding objective of the program in the first few weeks was to actually model the first step of the learning framework: providing an open-ended opportunity for students (teachers) to interact with purposely selected materials and to generate questions and hypotheses from working with the readings. During this time, teachers had the opportunity to post their questions on discussion boards so others could comment and assist in the formulation and refinement of questions and hypotheses.

Teachers were paired in small groups of two or three and asked to have further interaction (via email and private discussion) regarding the nature of constructivist teaching and learning. The specific direction given by the course instructors (principal and professor) was to identify the differences between traditional and constructivist instruction, and have serious dialogue about the strengths and weaknesses of these teaching strategies in the area of technology.

Discoveries made during this initial step of the course included a realization that constructivist teaching does not involve a complete change in how teachers deliver instruction, and that much of what they considered "traditional" could be incorporated into a more "constructivist" delivery. For example, the traditional lecture format is a crucial component of the first step in the framework: presenting material and information that provides an opportunity for students (teachers) to question and explore their thoughts. The group discovered the importance of presenting a lesson in a traditional lecture format before sending students to computer workstations.

Middle Few Weeks

During this time, the course content and direction focused on Step 2 of the learning cycle: introduce concepts more complex and sophisticated that perhaps were involved in the discussion and interaction of the first few weeks. The goal was to move to the next level, and demonstrate how technology can assist in this transition. The following concept was introduced (again, online) to the teachers, having a direct implication for school leadership:

> Technology use in the classroom can influence and be influenced by leadership. Leadership itself may be transformed as a result of interaction with technology and staff. Presumably, leaders will need to play a more active role in monitoring the instruction that fosters the effective use of technology in our schools. How can the educational leader (i.e., principal) determine how technology is used, what it can do, and ultimately, its contribution to student performance. (Avolio, 2000)

The introduction of this concept was guided by several objectives, encouraging teachers to do the following:

1. Interact with the principal regarding the role of leadership in technology.

2. Consider the concept of leadership and technology influencing each other.

3. Draw attention to the support (financial and philosophical) necessary from leadership if technology is to have an impact on teaching and learning.

Here's an example of one teacher's interaction with the principal on the discussion board:

"I think technology implementation can suffer from too much leadership as it can from too little. Sometimes a principal displays total control over technology because it is his or her agenda. Often, principals don't solicit input from staff. At one end you may have the principal who does not accept the role of leadership with technology implementation and appoints a person or committee (often non-instructional) to control the use of technology. At the other end, you may have a principal with her own agenda, diverting technology from serving the needs of the entire staff and student body."

Can you see the higher-level thinking here, and the value of including the principal in the dialogue?

Last Several Weeks

Recall Step 3 of the Atkins and Karplus learning cycle: concept application. Before I address this part of the process, let me remind you that the first two steps (discovery and concept introduction) often involve several repeating sequences of each before moving on to Step 3.

During concept application, students (teachers) work on new problems with the potential for evoking a fresh look at the concepts previously studied (Brooks & Brooks, 1993). The culminating activity for the course involves teams of three (two teachers, one principal) designing an instructional unit in any content area and implementing the use of technology. Included in the design were references to the 12 principles of constructivist teaching and activities covering each. Notice that the principal's role in this activity was crucial if not a bit overwhelming: The principal participated as a member of each of the small groups.

Constructivists believe students (teachers) should work on problems and situations simulating and representing authentic tasks. For this reason, teachers in the course were asked to implement the instructional unit in the classroom during that current semester. The assessment would involve a discussion with the principal and teachers at the end of the implementation phase.

DESIGN EFFECTIVE TECHNOLOGY STAFF DEVELOPMENT PROGRAMS

I hope these examples of how we tie constructivist principles to the use of technology in the classroom will help you as you begin to plan staff development activities in your own school. Though we may be in agreement about the value and strength of constructivist learning theory, we must be cognizant of the fact that staff development programs must match individual school site needs with available resources utilizing an effective delivery method. Clearly, we must guard against adopting "canned" methods or strategies. Only through assessing the needs of your staff, their expertise and deficiencies, and considering your available resources, can you hope to create a method of delivering appropriate and sustaining professional development in technology.

Think for a moment about the existing staff development methods used in your school or district. If they are anything like the methods observed in most schools, they are heavily focused on workshops, with an occasional outside speaker from a nearby college or university. We have a tendency to select activities without considering how they help to meet the goals and objectives of our school. Existing technology staff development is no exception. Much of it consists of "hit and miss" workshops related to hardware and/or software, with little tie to instructional theory and even less to what will help students achieve. Before we leave this thought, let me present the National Education Association Research Division's suggested 19 methods of staff development program delivery:

1. Classes and courses
2. Institutes
3. Conferences
4. Workshops
5. Staff meetings
6. Committee work
7. Professional reading
8. Field trips
9. Travel
10. Individual conferences
11. Camping
12. Work experience
13. Teacher exchanges
14. Research
15. Professional writing
16. Cultural experiences
17. Professional association work
18. Visits and demonstrations
19. Community organizational work

Using our model of connecting technology use to constructivist teaching, the list above provides myriad opportunities for designing effective, productive (and fun) staff development programs for the use of technology to improve instruction.

CONCLUDING THOUGHTS

David Pepi and Geoffrey Scheurman from the University of Wisconsin (1996) draw three parallels between Hans Christian Andersen's tale *The Emperor's New Clothes* and our headlong rush to maximize the use of computer technology in public school classrooms. Remember the story?

> Two charlatans hoodwinked the Emperor and his court by claiming they could weave the most beautiful cloth in the world. Interested in keeping up with the latest fashions, the Emperor hired the so-called weavers and supplied them with the gold metals and silk threads they claimed they needed to weave the magnificent cloth. As the weeks passed, the weavers called for more and more gold and silk thread. Instead of using any of the gold or thread for weaving, they squandered the money on themselves. When presenting the "non-existent" clothes to the Emperor, they explained that they had magical powers and could be seen by ordinary folks. It took a child, free of the burden of self-doubt to shout, *But the Emperor has nothing on at all!!* (Andersen, 1949, p. 41)

Pepi and Scheurman's three parallels to our use of technology in schools are these:

1. Like the Emperor, education has a long history of gravitating toward the latest fashion, often at great cost to the profession and those it serves.

2. Just as in the weaving of magic cloth, computer technology takes money. With money comes power, and power can corrupt (consider the percentage of money allocated for technology in our operating budgets).

3. The lure of computer technology has a magic air about it. Faced with silvery disks with rainbow hues and an abstract highway that makes the yellow brick road seem mundane, the uninitiated may find it hard to question the legitimacy of the movement, much less say to no or whoa to it. (p. 230)

Closing this chapter on staff development with a quote from Philip Schlechty's *Inventing Better Schools* (1997) seems appropriate:

Whether the present demand that our schools be restructured will be positively responded to remains to be seen. But I am confident of one thing: Without leaders who will stay the course and without staff developers who understand what leads men and women to the frontier in the first place and what these men and women need to keep on going, all our efforts to reform our schools will fail. (p. 220)

CHAPTER SIX

Resisters
and Saboteurs

Dealing With Teachers Resistant
to Technology Implementation

Ever so eloquently, Phillip Schlechty (1997) discusses five types of actors participating in any change process. It is important for school leaders to understand these different actors and their needs, desires, and roles in the process of any implementation of program development.

Every school has *trailblazers:* teachers and staff who willingly venture into the unknown, such as the implementation of technology. Education leaders are remiss if they do not provide opportunities for trailblazers to be out in front of innovation efforts. *Pioneers,* though as adventurous as trailblazers, need assurance that the program implementation is worth the effort. *Settlers,* the third type of actors, need more detail and more specific direction than do either trailblazers or pioneers.

Resisters (called *stay-at-homes* by Schlechty) are simply satisfied with the status quo and see no reason to change their thinking or strategies for doing things. Though the principal must provide opportunities for resisters to see the advantages of the program implementation, resisters are generally not a threat to innovation. The danger of course is to neglect resisters, for fear that they will join forces with the fifth group of actors, the *saboteurs.*

OH, THOSE PESKY RESISTERS (AND TYRANTS, TIME BOMBERS, SNIPERS, BACK-STABBERS, UNDERMINERS, CONNIVERS, PLOTTERS, AND RUMOR MONGERS)!

Most dangerous and detrimental to efforts to implement new programs to improve teaching and learning are the *saboteurs:* those teachers who not only aren't interested in new programs, but are actually committed to stopping new ideas such as technology implementation. Saboteurs can stop innovation in its tracks. They are very astute at knowing how best to change directions—even by enlisting support from other staff, community, and board members. Schlechty posits that "the best place to have saboteurs is on the inside where they can be watched rather than on the outside where they can cause trouble without it being detected until the effects have been felt" (p. 218).

BUT TO IGNORE THEM IS A DRASTIC MISTAKE

For any movement of change to take place successfully and have a positive impact on teaching and learning, a large number of faculty and staff must be involved. To think we can move ahead with just the *trailblazers* and *pioneers* is exactly why so many of our reform efforts fail.

If we look closely at our resisters and saboteurs, we recognize that many of them, as Schlechty points out, have the same characteristics as the trailblazers and pioneers. Many may reveal a past as trailblazers, but began resisting due to a lack of leadership, or more than likely worked with leaders who did not give them support and encouragement and trust. Herein lies a paradox: Though resisters display immediate opposition, they possess untapped energy and creativity often ignored by leaders.

Two quotes from the business world seem appropriate here:

"Had there not been resistance, I don't think we would have been as successful as we have been. That being said, I hated that resistance." (Patrick Connolly, Executive Vice President, Williams-Sonoma Company)

"We must find the radicals, the true revolutionaries, and support them." (Louis V. Gerstner, Jr., Chairman and CEO, IBM)

THEY APPEAR WHEN LEAST EXPECTED

Even if you have incorporated everyone (including the resisters) in the planning process, there will still be resistance down the road. In my experience, the resisters surface after the beginning of the implementation, just when the project is ready to go. During the planning stages, technology implementation is just thinking out loud, and resisters are not yet convinced the change will occur. As your technology plan starts to look as if it will be implemented, the threat to those who oppose it increases as the impact of the implementation becomes clear. So, a "heads up" to principals as technology leaders! The resisters and saboteurs will most often appear after the implementation process has begun. Also, remember resisters and saboteurs can surface from both the internal and external environment.

POTENTIAL REASONS FOR RESISTANCE AND SABOTAGE

Let's look at some of the reasons why certain faculty might resist or sabotage the implementation of technology in our schools. Each of these (and any others that may surface) must be addressed in our planning and implementation efforts. Some common reasons for resistance are as follows:

1. Some teachers feel they do not possess the adequate skills to implement technology in their classroom. Complicating the matter further for the principal as technology leader is the fact that many of these teachers are reluctant or embarrassed to admit this feeling of inadequacy—it is far easier to simply refuse or resist.

2. Several teachers (even in today's technological world) are not yet convinced of the benefits or value of technology to support teaching and learning. As with anything, if someone

does not believe in its value, why would that person support the program or concept?

3. It is not uncommon to hear teachers express concern and personal fear that technology may soon begin to replace faculty. In an earlier chapter, I shared my previous experience with technology implementation and noted that a significant resister (and saboteur) was the local teachers' union (internal threat), some of whose members believed that teaching positions might be in jeopardy if technology programs were implemented.

In Moss Kanter's insightful book, *Evolve* (2001), she discusses her list of reasons people resist change in the early stages of implementation, and the importance of leaders to work around them. Though her discussion is not specifically about technology implementation in our schools, I think her reasons are very appropriate to share with you here:

1. *Loss of face:* Fear that dignity will be undermined, a place of honor removed; embarrassment because the change feels like exposure for past mistakes

2. *Loss of control:* Anger at decisions being taken out of one's hands, power shifting elsewhere

3. *Excess uncertainty:* Feeling uninformed about where the change will lead, what is coming next—a sensation like walking off a cliff blindfolded

4. *Surprise, surprise:* Automatic defensiveness—no advanced warning, no chance to get ready

5. *The "difference" effect:* Rejection of the change because it doesn't fit the existing mental models, seems strange and unfamiliar, and challenges usually unquestioned habits and routines

6. *"Can I do it?"* Concerns about future competence, worries about whether one will still be successful after the change

7. *Ripple effects:* Annoyance at disruptions to other activities and interference with the accomplishment of unrelated tasks

8. *More work:* Resistance to additional things to do, new things to learn, and no time to do it all

9. *Past resentments:* Memories of past hostilities or problems that were never resolved

10. *Real threats:* Anger that the change will inflict real pain and create real losers

Not wanting to bore you with the management/leadership dichotomy we are all so familiar with, I think there is a parallel here. I suspect what Moss Kanter is getting at is the fact that the principal as technology leader must not get too wrapped up in the management of change to the exclusion of dealing with the more human side—leadership through respecting and understanding what people feel and believe about issues. In addition, what are their fears and why do they feel threatened by technology implementation?

The nature of the beast is that technology is so naturally impersonal and technical it invites a neglect of the more human side of change. The principal as technology leader must be careful that he or she is not consumed by the management of technology at the expense of working through (not around) teachers' fears and emotions.

THE NEED FOR A SIGNIFICANT NUMBER OF FACULTY

Without evidence or empirical data to support this, I believe one reason for a lack of involvement and commitment from segments of faculty is directly related to a misunderstanding of what effective use of technology really means. Too many of our colleagues still equate technology with computers in classrooms and have yet to move beyond this thinking. Moss Kanter clearly warns, "Most people still imagine that technology in schools means computers in classrooms—but, that is the least important, and often most counterproductive application of technology, fostering individual isolation" (p. 25).

In order to implement technology effectively, the principal as technology leader must strive to include as many faculty as possible in the process. Think about other innovations or programs in our schools that may have been successful—cooperative learning strategies, site-based decision making, and inclusion of special needs students, among others. *No innovation or program has been successfully implemented without the involvement and commitment of a significant portion of faculty.* I am not suggesting the successful implementation of technology is simple. But one or two teachers here and there, as powerful as these folks are, will not result in the highest impact, most productive application of technology to improve teaching and learning.

We must be careful not to create "in-groups" and "out-groups" and avoid the temptation to be satisfied with a few teachers or staff members on board. The priority agenda for the principal as technology leader is to encourage and support wide-based involvement and commitment to technology use in our schools. OK, but let's be specific: How might one accomplish such a feat?

TIPS FOR REACHING A SIGNIFICANT PORTION OF FACULTY (INCLUDING THE RESISTERS AND SABOTEURS)

1. First and foremost, the principal as technology leader must involve all stakeholders (teachers, parents, students, board members, business partners) in the dialogue and seek consensus on the true value of technology. No, it is not about *boxes and wires*. Ends (curricular goals and objectives) must guide the means (technology), not the other way around, as so often happens in today's schools. This dialogue takes time, but must involve everyone and preface any aggressive move toward further planning or implementation. Such forums for dialogue include faculty meetings, informal discussion with teachers, invitations to union representatives, addressing Lions and Rotary Clubs, boards of education, and others. Empowering people to understand information resources and technology is one of the major challenges confronting instructional designers.

Whether a technology program succeeds is greatly influenced by the way teachers and others think about teaching, learning, and the role of technology.

2. We discussed earlier the realization that each school or district likely has several teachers who have the potential to push technology implementation forward or can choose to stop it in its tracks. To increase the chance of keeping these teachers on board, focus your discussions on curriculum benefits rather than the technical aspects of technology. Emphasizing the technical "bells and whistles" is not only counterproductive, but also has a tendency to alienate certain segments of the faculty. Instead, focus on connecting technology with existing instructional strategies used by faculty. And emphasize the power of technology to help us with our agreed on goals and objectives regarding student learning.

3. Extensive teacher education (vs. training) in the integration of technology into the curriculum is not only needed but required. As discussed earlier, though training in basic technological skills is necessary, major emphasis should be placed on a more important aspect of using technology in education: addressing beliefs and dispositions about how technology can improve teaching and learning.

CONCLUDING THOUGHTS

Concerning the resistant employee and disagreement in the organization, Champy (1996) states,

> A culture that squashes disagreement is a culture doomed to stagnate, because change always begins with disagreement. Besides, disagreement can never be squashed entirely. It gets repressed, to emerge later as a pervasive sense of injustice, followed by apathy, resentment, and even sabotage. (p. 82)

Innovation and change often freeze because principals and other leaders fail to learn from those who disagree with us. We must change our thinking about resistance: It is not only likely to occur but must be viewed as necessary and a positive component of change. Disagreement and resistance can make a positive contribution to the implementation of technology in our schools. Maurer (1996), in a book entitled *Beyond the Wall of Resistance*, reminds us,

> Often those who resist have something important to tell us. People resist for what they feel are good reasons. They may see alternatives we never dreamed of. They may understand problems about the minutiae of implementation that we never see from our lofty perch atop Mount Olympus. (p. 49)

Herein lies the power of including the thoughts of all and the danger of heading off with a small group of like-minded teachers committed to technology. In my experience with new programs and innovation, rarely has a small, select group of faculty had a significant influence on the resisters and saboteurs. To the contrary, the results have created further resistance and resentment between the in-group and the out-group.

CHAPTER SEVEN

Teacher Evaluation and the Use of Technology

IMPORTANCE OF ASSESSING TEACHER PERFORMANCE

The tasks and responsibilities of a school principal, though often daunting, certainly include the assurance that "excellence in teaching" is the centerpiece of the district's agenda. Supervision of the instructional process is the "quality control" element of student learning, and teacher evaluation is a vital component of that quality control, as well as an important element of effective leadership by the principal. When a teacher is performing in a marginally effective manner and the principal does not confront the teacher with the problem, then the principal is also performing in a marginal manner (Smith, 1998).

We currently appraise the performance of teachers for the following reasons, among others:

1. Appraisal fosters the self-development of each teacher.

2. Appraisal helps to identify a variety of tasks that the teacher is capable of performing.

3. Appraisal helps to identify staff development needs.

4. Appraisal helps to improve performance.

5. Appraisal helps to determine the placement, transfer, or promotion of a teacher.

6. Appraisal helps to determine if a teacher should be retained in the district. (Rebore, 1998, p. 221)

EVALUATING TECHNOLOGY USE IN THE CLASSROOM

I do not argue with our commitment to the appropriate use of effective teaching appraisal practices. What seems to be missing, however, is the inclusion of the same rigorous attention to evaluating technology use in the classroom. In addition, many educators mistakenly believe that effective technology integration correlates with how much hardware and software is available in the classroom and/or our labs. I will go even further and suggest that even the "use" of available technology by all students does not necessarily translate to effective technology integration. *It's really about how the teacher uses technology to support clearly defined learning objectives.*

Consider this: When we visit a classroom to observe a language arts lesson, do we measure effective teaching and learning solely by the number of language arts textbooks available and whether or not teachers and students are using them? Visiting an algebra lesson, are we satisfied with the teacher's performance if students are using the adopted text along with the new calculators purchased by the district? Certainly not. Why? *Curriculum standards and learning objectives* are in place for our language arts and math curriculums, and both teachers and principals are aware of them. I am not convinced that we evaluate the effective use of technology with the same rigorous kind of standards and learning objectives. Technology that does not advance student learning has little value in the classroom, and I suggest even "gets in the way" of other types of learning. Technology linked to standards and agreed-on learning objectives can help all students achieve at high levels.

SO WHAT DO I LOOK FOR?

If technology integration is not about hardware and software or even necessarily the use of it, then what is it and what do I look for in a classroom observation? First of all, let's look at the research and utilize some resources already available to us. No need to reinvent the wheel.

Most of us are familiar with the regional educational laboratories, the national development system administered by the Office of Educational Research and Development, U.S. Department of Education. These regional educational laboratories provide communities with the latest information on learning. Recently, one of the regional labs examined how various educational technologies can increase teacher effectiveness and improve student achievement.

The North Central Regional Educational Laboratory (NCREL) recently pulled together the latest information on how students learn best and compiled it in a guide to those technologies that are most useful in promoting student learning. The publication, *Plugging In: Choosing and Using Educational Technology* (North Central Regional Educational Laboratory, 1995), introduces what we know about effective learning and effective technology, and puts it together in a planning framework for educational leaders and policymakers. I strongly recommend this resource for your individual planning at your school site. I will be referring to parts of this document as we discuss things to look for (and things you don't want to see) in the classroom as you focus on the integration of technology.

MEANINGFUL, ENGAGED LEARNING

In recent years, researchers have formed a strong consensus on the importance of engaged learning in schools and classrooms. This consensus, together with a recognition of the changing needs of 21st-century students, has stimulated the development of specific indicators that can act as a guide in applying a set of standards and learning objectives to the implementation of technology. The indicators used by NCREL were developed by Jones, Valdez, Nowakowski, and Rasmussen (1995), who suggest that technology

Figure 7.1. NCREL learning and technology framework.

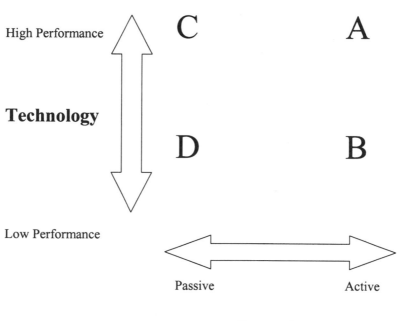

SOURCE: Credit is given for this model to NCREL and Jones, Valdez, Nowakowski, and Rasmussen (1995).

effectiveness can be defined as the intersection of two continuums shown in Figure 7.1.

When the two continuums are combined, four learning and technology patterns result:

A. Engaged learning and high technology performance
B. Engaged learning and low technology performance
C. Passive learning and high technology performance
D. Passive learning and low technology performance

The authors developed a set of learning indicators to help planners concentrate on moving instruction from passive learning to active learning. In addition, they developed a set of technology indicators to assist with keeping technology learning at a high performance level. They strongly encourage schools to focus their vision for using technology primarily in Categories A and B.

Let's look at how we might use the *learning indicators* and *technology indicators* to effectively evaluate and assess the use of technology in the classroom. Using NCREL's indicators of engaged learning, we can create a framework for designing effective evaluation tools for classroom observation of technology implementation. The real value of this procedure is the movement away from passive and low technology performance levels and toward more active and high technology performance levels. For example, NCREL's model includes "Teacher Roles" as one of the indicators for engaged learning.

Certainly, effective classroom instruction is dependent on exactly how the teacher interacts with students. As simplistic as this sounds, it draws attention to the importance of expecting teachers to be *facilitators, guides, co-learners, and co-investigators* in the instructional process. The following section displays NCREL's indicator of "Teacher Roles" intersecting with high performance technology indicators.

Teacher Roles for Engaged Learning

Facilitator. The teacher provides rich environments, experiences, and activities for learning by incorporating opportunities for collaborative work, problem solving, authentic tasks, and shared knowledge and responsibility.

Guide. In a collaborative classroom, the teacher must act as a guide—a complex and varied role that incorporates mediation, modeling, and coaching. When mediating student learning, the teacher frequently adjusts the level of information and support based on students' needs and helps students to link new information with prior knowledge, refine their problem-solving strategies, and learn how to learn.

Co-Learner and Co-Investigator. Teachers and students participate in investigations with practicing professionals. Using this model, students explore new frontiers and become producers of knowledge in knowledge-building communities. With the help of technology, students may become the teachers and teachers become the learners.

DESIGNING A GUIDE FOR CLASSROOM OBSERVATION AND TEACHER EVALUATION

Using the learning/technology indicators above, let's compile a list of questions that can serve as a guide or framework in assessing the teacher's role with technology in the classroom.

Facilitator

1. Is the teacher interacting with students using computers or other technology in the room? Or are students working without collaboration from the teacher other students?

2. As students work with technology, is the teacher supervising, monitoring, and facilitating students' project work, posing questions, and suggesting responses as appropriate?

Guide

1. Does the teacher simply give directions on how to complete assignments with technology? Or is there evidence of further interaction focusing on helping students to refine their problem-solving strategies and connecting new information to prior knowledge?

2. Is the teacher "leading from the front" or "guiding from the side"?

Co-Learner and Co-Investigator

1. Is the teacher's expertise and instructional delivery domineering? Or are the students' individual interests and expertise blended with those of the teacher, allowing for teacher learning along with students?

2. Is there evidence of the involvement of other professionals, such as technology coordinators, media specialists, and librarians encouraging knowledge-building communities?

Connecting what we already know about effective learning (engagement, activity, collaboration) with the implementation and use of technology in the classroom (or lab) assists the instructional leader (principal) in managing and sustaining effective technology curricula in our schools. Most important, connecting learning and technology in this way helps us monitor the appropriate use of technology to improve student learning. We must move away from technology skills taught in isolation and closer to purposive integration of technology across the entire curriculum and learning environment.

TEACHER ROLES, OK—BUT WHAT ABOUT STUDENT ROLES?

We now have an idea of what the teacher's role might look like when observing technology use in the classroom, but let's take a look at one more of NCREL's learning indicators—student roles for engaged learning—and add to our questions serving as a framework for instructional supervision of teaching and learning in the classroom (Jones et al., 1995).

Student Roles for Engaged Learning

Explorer. Students discover concepts, connections, and skills by interacting with the physical world, materials, technology, and other people. Such discovery-oriented exploration provides students with opportunities to make decisions while figuring out the components/attributes of events, objects, people, and concepts.

Cognitive Apprentice. Students become cognitive apprentices when they observe, apply, and refine through practice the thinking processes used by real-world practitioners. In this model, students reflect on their thinking processes in diverse situations and across a range of tasks, and they articulate the common elements of their experiences.

Producers of Knowledge. Students generate products for themselves and their community that synthesize and integrate knowledge and skills. For example, students use technology applications to make presentations both at school and in the community. Through the use of technology, students are increasingly able to make significant contributions to the world's knowledge.

ADDING TO OUR QUESTIONS GUIDING TECHNOLOGY SUPERVISION

As we did with the teacher roles for engaged learning, we'll generate a few questions focusing on student roles for effecting learning. As before, we are attempting to connect what we already know about effective learning (engagement, activity, collaboration) with classroom use of technology.

Explorer

1. Are students using technology (computers, etc.) to increase their knowledge of historical events, world news, and other people outside the classroom? Or are they using technology primarily for drill and practice activities or the remediation of existing skills and knowledge?

2. Is there evidence of students' use of e-mail and the Internet to communicate with experts or researchers outside the classroom?

Cognitive Apprentice

3. Are students exposed, through the use of technology, to appropriate experts who provide models and feedback from outside the classroom? Or does modeling and feedback only come from the teacher?

4. Are students involved in programs outside of the school such as school-to-careers activities with area businesses and community service agencies?

Producers of Knowledge

5. Is there evidence, in or out of the classroom, of computer-produced projects such as research reports, speeches, and other written compositions?

6. Is there evidence, in and out of the classroom, of pictures, graphs, or other graphic products produced by technology (computer, video recorder, digital camera)?

CLASSROOM OBSERVATION AND TEACHER EVALUATION: WHAT'S THE BIG DEAL?

Paraphrasing Emerson, Pepi and Scheurman (1996) state, "computer technology is in the saddle and it is riding us" (p. 229). The principal charged with instructional leadership and monitoring the delivery of instruction must not get caught up in letting technology use in the classroom exist with no connection to what we know about teaching and learning. Technology must coexist with constructivist principles of learning (see Chapter 5).

Too often, teachers use the computer as a tool for drill and practice, or worse, "like television in the hands of many lazy instructors as an instrument for classroom management" (Pepi & Scheurman, 1996, p. 231). Hours spent on the Internet may result in a good amount of *incidental learning*, but the activity is often used by teachers as a way of keeping students on task, rather than as a tool to construct knowledge.

The evaluation process provides an opportunity to stimulate student achievement, and also to improve teacher performance. Principals need first to understand how technology supports the curriculum and learning objectives, and second, to help teachers determine effective strategies for connecting technology with the most recent research and development findings on learning. *We must be certain that technology wears the saddle and we are riding it!*

CHAPTER EIGHT

Sustaining Effective Technology Plans

Management and Leadership

A s important as wise planning and successful implementation are, it is the issue of sustainability that separates educationally sound, effective technology programs from ineffective ones. What are the strategies necessary to keep programs alive, moving forward, and connected to increased student achievement? Sustaining effective technology programs (as defined by your individual school or district) is not unlike sustaining any other effective education program. What's required is a principal with the knowledge, skills, and dispositions (i.e., beliefs) to do so. OK, you might say, but do I concentrate on *managing* the program or *leading* the program?

MANAGEMENT AND LEADERSHIP: A DICHOTOMY IN THEORY OR PRACTICE?

It is unfortunate indeed that university professors, authors of school administration textbooks, and other authors of leadership theory such as Bolman and Deal (1997), Peters and Waterman (1982), and Sergiovani (1996), "preach" the distinction between management and leadership characteristics. The result has been our misguided interpretation and belief that the two require entirely discrete, separate qualities.

My experience, and likely your own, involved two years of preparatory coursework emphasizing the virtues and necessity of effective leadership skills such as the ability to develop visions and mission statements. I then found myself immersed in the world of school administration consisting mostly of management duties such as budget maintenance, meetings, staff development, and so forth.

Those of us working on the "front line" of school administration know full well that effective principals function best with an appropriate and balanced blend of both management and leadership skills. Looking closely at *ineffective* leaders (Davis, 1998), we find an unbalanced mixture, heavy on one side or the other.

So, what are leadership and management characteristics? And what is their relationship to effective implementation and sustainability of technology programs in our schools? My contention, as stated earlier, is that leading and managing technology programs is no different than leading and managing a good math program or a good reading program. For whatever reasons, we have been led to believe that leading technology programs must be more mysterious and complex than what we do every day in our jobs. Similarly, our strategy for sustaining an effective technology program should be no different than our strategy for sustaining an effective kindergarten reading program. Let me now offer some clarification of leadership and management skills, and their relationship to planning and sustaining technology programs.

DICHOTOMY OR CONNECTIBILITY?

I agree that distinguishing between the two constructs of leadership and management is useful (and necessary). The problem, however, is that we in this profession dwell so heavily on the dichotomy, we lose sight of the absolute requirement that the two be interconnected and equally present: Effective school leadership requires a continuous blend and balance of both leadership and management.

Let's look at the research for a moment. Admitting that we have lessons to learn from business and other areas of leadership, let's focus on the expertise of specific researchers in the field of educational administration. Through the work of the National Association of Elementary School Principals (NAESP), the National Association of Secondary School Principals (NASSP), and the American Association of School Administrators (AASA), characteristics of effective school leadership have been defined and agreed on. And yes, some are considered leadership skills and others considered management skills. But this is exactly the point: Though a distinction is made, the contention of interconnectivity is paramount. Box 8.1 shows the individual constructs accompanied by a definition.

Though the individual definitions are displayed in Box 8.1, we really want to know what an effective leader looks like "in action." If we observe an effective technology program leader, what might we see? For example, if we observe effective planning, how do we know if the leader is "defining purpose and setting organizational goals"? Fortunately, the education administration researchers have come to the rescue. Box 8.1 reveals what we call "look-fors" under each leadership construct. The "look-fors" are the important "on-the-job" behaviors that help sustain effective technology programs. Though I include only two "look-fors" associated with each of the 12 leadership constructs in Box 8.2, you can find a more detailed list in Resource B.

With the use of Box 8.2, and perhaps Resource B, relate each of the five look-fors associated with each leadership construct and ask yourself, "Would this behavior apply to the management, leadership, and sustainability of my strategic technology plan?" I suggest that every single one is applicable. This strategy has two significant strengths that help sustain your technology plan: (a) It keeps you, the building principal, as the instructional leader in all areas of instruction, and (b) it assures that you, as building principal, lead and manage the technology plan in the same student-oriented manner that you lead and manage other aspects of your leadership. Perhaps the most important element of this strategy is that it keeps the technology plan related to all other areas of instruction. Recall the belief of Cheryl Lemke that there is danger in planning for technology in isolation: Technology should be an important component of the overall school improvement plan.

Box 8.1   Constructs of Effective Principal Leadership

Planning: Defines purpose and sets organizational goals

Organizing: Defines tasks to be completed in various activities and sequential events

Problem solving: Analyzes problems effectively and reaches logical conclusions

Creativity: Demonstrates innovation and inventiveness in work-related situations

Decisiveness: Renders timely, appropriate decisions, and accepts the consequences

Systems analysis: Understands educational systems in the effective functioning of operational components

Vision: Possesses a clear and positive view of the past, present, and future of the school

Communications: Processes messages with precise understanding

Instructional leadership: Works effectively with the school community to advance student learning

Group leadership and team building: Mobilizes others to collaborate in accomplishing school goals

Climate development: Shapes the psychosocial environment of the school to promote accomplishment of the mission

Instructional supervision: Works effectively with teachers to improve instruction

---

PUTTING IT ALL TOGETHER

Although I digressed from our discussion of technology to spend time talking about management and leadership in general, I hope you agree that, with our leadership framework in hand, it will be much easier to develop strategies for managing and sustaining

Box 8.2   Leadership Constructs and Matching "Look-Fors"

PLANNING

1. Encourages staff in planning and goal establishment
2. Involves stakeholders in the planning process

ORGANIZING

1. Breaks larger tasks into smaller, manageable activities
2. Assists group members in defining tasks to be completed

PROBLEM SOLVING

1. Clarifies the problem with others before drawing a conclusion
2. Collects and analyzes essential information logically before reaching a conclusion to a problem

CREATIVITY

1. Suggests innovative means to accomplish organizational objectives
2. Provides innovative suggestions to faculty and staff in handling educational issues

DECISIVENESS

1. Distinguishes between urgent decisions and those that can be postponed
2. Reaches decisions logically and in a timely fashion

SYSTEMS ANALYSIS

1. Encourages the faculty and staff to invest in systems thinking and organizational outcomes
2. Retains a sense of overall mission and goals

VISION

1. Seeks to develop and continuously modify a shared vision of the school
2. Nurtures partnership of teachers and parents to advance school vision

COMMUNICATIONS

1. Expresses clear and concise language in communiqués
2. Exhibits sensitivity toward diverse populations in communications

INSTRUCTIONAL LEADERSHIP

1. Articulates high expectations for student learning
2. Demonstrates interest in student learning by maintaining a visible presence in the classrooms

GROUP LEADERSHIP AND TEAM BUILDING

1. Establishes a framework for collaborative group action
2. Uses perspectives and strengths of individual group members

CLIMATE DEVELOPMENT

1. Ensures a safe environment for learning
2. Works effectively with diverse elements of the school community

INSTRUCTIONAL SUPERVISION

1. Conducts frequent teacher evaluations
2. Maintains expertise of alternative instructional practices

our strategic technology plan. In this last section, I will demonstrate an effective strategy for taking what we already know about effective leadership and applying it to technology program sustainability.

I will use the same 12 constructs of leadership and the corresponding look-fors to develop a specific leadership framework for technology. Box 8.3 shows the procedure using the first construct, *planning*. You will notice that I am applying the same look-fors mentioned earlier in the chapter, but reworded to fit my goals for technology.

Notice that each of these two look-fors covers a different area. The first one addresses bringing all stakeholders from both the

---

Box 8.3   Adapting Technology to the Construct of Planning

PLANNING

1. Involve all stakeholders (i.e., teachers, staff, parents, students, business leaders, community members) in the initial and subsequent planning for effective technology programs to increase student learning.
2. Encourage staff (including *resisters* and *saboteurs*) in planning and setting program goals and objectives.

---

internal and *external* school community together to help decide on the general direction for technology in our school or district. Relating back to the first of the three components of strategic planning (i.e., Where do we want to go?), we see this that this group of stakeholders looks at the question in a general way. The second look-for involves working with the *internal* staff (i.e., teachers, curriculum directors, etc.) to develop more specific and detailed plans, guided by the more general plan developed by the first group. For example, if the first group identifies "reducing the use of games and drill and practice activities" as a direction, the internal stakeholders group must decide on appropriate and effective strategies to get there.

Just a note regarding the inclusion of resisters and saboteurs. In too many instances these folks are skipped. Think for a moment! Resisters and saboteurs are less likely to continue their resistance and sabotage if they are actively involved and respected in the planning process. At least if their negative activities continue, they are visible to everyone rather than behind the scenes. Guaranteed? No, but the alternative—disregarding their input—is a guarantee of program failure.

Let's now build another leadership construct into our technology plan. I choose *instructional leadership* to emphasize the importance of holding student results and outcomes in our technology program to the same high standard of accountability as we do in math, science, reading, and our arts programs. As building principal, you know that effective instructional leadership is critical to

---

Box 8.4   Adapting Technology to the Construct of Instructional Leadership

---

INSTRUCTIONAL LEADERSHIP

1. Articulates high expectations for student learning through the use of technology.
2. Demonstrates interest in student learning through the use of technology by maintaining a visible presence in the classrooms.

---

student achievement. It is equally critical to the success of our technology programs.

I will not belabor the issue here, but simply point out a key component to sustaining effective technology programs: We must tie the use of technology to student achievement in all content areas. We must get beyond thinking of technology as hardware and software. And we must, as leaders, be committed to regularly monitoring and assessing technology use in the same ways we monitor and assess other aspects of the curriculum. Box 8.4 addresses two look-fors in the area of instructional leadership.

You see how we are integrating our established high standards for student achievement with similar high expectations for technology in the classroom? Herein lies the strength of using our instructional leadership "look-fors" for sustaining high-quality technology programs focused on teaching and learning. As I've emphasized throughout this book, principals as technology leaders must not allow the use of technology to "sit in the saddle," but rather insist that technology coexist with our curriculum and our already agreed-on high standards for teaching and learning.

The second look-for in Box 8.4 focuses on teacher and classroom observation. I'm sure we agree on the importance of principal visibility in the classroom when it concerns any other aspect of the instructional program (e.g., math, language arts, science, and social science). Why not assume the same importance of observing teaching and learning as it pertains to technology use in the classroom?

We will not take the time (or space) to adapt the remaining 10 leadership constructs and their accompanying look-fors for inclusion in your technology planning process. You are encouraged, however, to complete the process yourself as you proceed with your technology planning. Also, keep in mind there is nothing *magical* about the number of look-fors included in Resource B. I displayed only two look-fors each for *planning* and *instructional supervision*, but would certainly include the other three in my plan for technology sustainability. And you could include many more: Add (or cautiously subtract) as you think appropriate to your own school or district technology plan.

CONCLUDING THOUGHTS

The focus of this chapter is to draw attention to the importance of using what we already know about effective leadership to design our plans for technology use. Research reveals that schools commonly leave out this important piece of the puzzle, resulting in isolated technology plans. Infusing existing components of effective leadership into your technology planning increases the likelihood that technology programs will be effectively managed, and more important, sustained.

CHAPTER NINE

The Future

Leadership and Technology Implementation

W ithout appropriate connection between leadership and technology implementation, potential exists for a *mishmash* of effects ranging from acceptance to resistance to rejection. This author argues that the introduction and implementation of technology in our schools create a simultaneous and reciprocal relationship with leadership in a variety of ways:

1. Leadership, as we presently know it, will likely experience further transformation and redefinition.

2. School environments are presently experiencing changes at a speed never witnessed before, and technology is at the very center of these changes—changes that require principals and other school leaders to make dramatic adjustments regarding effective leadership.

3. Though the principal's leadership plays a significant role in the successful implementation of technology, the *lack* of appropriate leadership can squander the educational potential of technology, creating environments that have little effect on teaching and learning, very often encouraging, reinforcing, and supporting more traditional strategies and practices such as drill and practice activities and electronic worksheets.

As if our profession needs a new buzzword, current researchers and writers in the field of leadership suddenly are referring to *e-leadership* (Avolio, 2000; Quinn-Mills, 2001). Harvard Business School professor Quinn-Mills contends that the core of *e-leadership* "requires leaders to identify those who are expert in the new technologies and support them, even stepping out of their way if necessary—to let new people point the direction giving them initiative—and to build an organizational framework (positions and culture) in which the new can replace the old" (p. v). Avolio (2000) discusses the interaction between technology and leadership and defines *e-leadership* as "a social influence process mediated by technology to produce a change in attitudes, feelings, thinking, behavior, and/or performance with individuals, groups, and/or organizations" (p. 4).

I suggest that because technology is so ubiquitous in our society and schools, effective leadership now must include leadership in technology. But it will be a mistake to view leadership in general and leadership in technology as dichotomous. Recall our discussion earlier about the difficulty we encountered when viewing leadership and management as two different constructs. We can make the same mistake here if we try to distinguish between leadership in general and leadership in technology. The point, and perhaps one I've belabored, is that the principal as technology leader blends the goals of technology implementation into the total mix of instructional leadership. This will maximize the benefits of technology and guard against separating the use of technology in our schools from a focus on the overall improvement of teaching and learning.

To help identify the nature and look of this new leadership, let's visit each of the three ways the implementation of technology creates a relationship with leadership, presented at the beginning of this chapter.

TECHNOLOGY LEADERSHIP DEFINED

First, I stated that because of the infusion of technology in our schools, leadership as we presently know it will experience further transformation. The gap between autocratic and participatory leadership must grow even wider if we are to successfully implement more and more technology in our schools. Even with our present use of participatory leadership in schools, one commonly sees *in-groups* and *out-groups* regarding technology use and implementation. Leaders who create (intentionally or unintentionally) an in-group and out-group "may see the best technology system blocked from effectively creating collaboration resulting from low levels of trust within the organization" (Avolio, 2000, p. 13).

In-groups are usually composed of technology consultants and coordinators partnered with teachers possessing adequate to exemplary skills and interest in using technology. On the other hand, those who either lack technical expertise or interest make up the out-group, and are not so visible, involved, or committed. This out-group can consist of veteran teachers lacking the skills or others who are not presently interested. For a variety of reasons, we have folks who are less likely to contribute in an active manner. Here is a caution: Many teachers, both trailblazers and saboteurs, do not respond over the noise of more active, talkative others. We often misinterpret this passive silence with indifference or lack of interest and commitment: Not necessarily! Of course, passive participants present a worthy challenge for the principal as technology leader, but one that will pay off. *The more variance of skills and interest a faculty possesses, the more participatory and collaborative the principal as technology leader must be.*

Philip Schlechty (1997), in his book entitled *Inventing Better Schools*, specifically addresses a redefined leadership for implementing technology in our schools:

> Supporting technological change requires much more than instituting workshops; it requires as well the creation of opportunities to practice and observe, and opportunities to be coached and coach others. When the effort to install technological changes fails, it is likely that leaders have simply not appreciated and provided for the quality of training and support that is needed.
>
> Or the effort may fail because of the fact that in schools, as in other organizations, technological changes often require structural changes, too. (p. 207)

Schlechty continues by pointing to the complexity involved in effective leadership and offers a more relevant and applicable definition of the role of principal as technology leader:

Systemic change, which usually involves procedural and technological changes as well, calls upon leaders to do all the things they must do to lead procedural and technological change—and more. It also calls on them to think, to conceptualize, to see relationships between and among events that might escape others, to help others see these relationships and overcome fear, and to assure, cajole, coach, and inspire hope. Most of all, systemic change calls upon leaders to be wise and sometimes demanding but always to be supportive of and reassuring to teachers. (p. 208)

CHANGES AT LIGHTNING SPEED

The second factor tying technology to leadership stated earlier relates to the speed of change we face in our schools. Constant change is part of our daily life in schools, but the fast-paced change accompanying computer technology in our schools is unlike any other change we have been involved with. The invention of the overhead projector was slow and gave us time to experiment with its use. The inclusion of television as an instructional tool was also a rather comfortable transition. However, computer technology is changing daily before our eyes. In my own arena of higher education, overnight (it seems), universities have started offering master's and doctoral programs entirely online. Teachers and administrators can now acquire state certification without even entering a classroom.

Moss Kanter calls it a spiral of increasing force: "The more technology is used, the more uses are identified, and the more it must be used to do more things. Change produces the need for more and deeper change" (2001, p. 231). What does this all have to do with the principal as technology leader? Let me explain.

The current change we are facing in our schools regarding technology implementation is different in pace, yes, but more important, it differs in respect to the number of people that must be involved in the change. Previous innovation and change encountered in our schools, such as shifts in learning theory, for instance, did not necessarily involve large numbers of faculty at one time. A teacher or two began implementing constructivist practices in the classroom, followed by a slow, methodical progression through other classrooms and grades. Technology implementation is a different kind of change. We are not asking small groups of teachers or grades to "give it a go." We are practically demanding that everyone participate, and not to take too much time in making the transition. Implications for the principal as technology leader? You bet.

Because the change associated with technology implementation is so rapid, it is not uncommon for principals as technology leaders to react too quickly. For example, it was not so long ago that yours truly, as superintendent of a school district in central California, recommended to the board of education the purchase of 50 state-of-the-art Macintosh computers, the Mac Plus model. A wonder these were supposed to be, with their 12-inch screens and 24K memory. I will not bore you with the rest of the story, except to tell you that in less than a year, these state-of-the-art machines became not-so-state-of-the-art. I never even took the time to ask if this new technology might be related to our teaching and learning goals and objectives. I was so swept up in the desire to fill up a lab with 50 computers, I did not take the time to consider how we would use the computers to encourage better teaching and student learning. (Remember, I stated earlier that my expertise in the area of technology implementation is accompanied by many scars from mistakes and errors.) My story relates to the important need for principals to understand and make clear to others the goals to be served by the change. In our obsession with being first, we began to fill our school with *hardware junkyards:* storerooms of Apple IIs, Mac Pluses, and Commodore computers, along with a wide variety of printers and other peripheral equipment. And let's not forget our *software junkyards—programs that soon became obsolete or worse, were never used at all.*

The technological changes we face currently, compared with the changes of the past, require much more attention to staff development and support. In this new era, as Schlechty so rightfully points out, "it is the obligation of leaders to ensure that those they lead know how to do what is expected of them" (p. 207). Our common practice of a workshop here and there, or a conference or two throughout the year, will not adequately help our faculty or ourselves to implement technology effectively and use it wisely. To the contrary, evidence reveals that too little and low quality staff development can actually do more harm than none at all. We cannot assume that teachers will learn how to effectively use technology to improve teaching and learning on their own, without appropriate support.

THE RISK OF SUPPORTING
TRADITIONAL PRACTICES

My third factor relating the implementation of technology to leadership focuses on the dangers of the lack of appropriate leadership. Principals as technology leaders have the greatest opportunity to radically influence teaching and learning. But *inappropriate* leadership might be more interested in supporting traditional instructional practices (e.g., excess use of drill and practice activities) than encouraging and supporting teachers to pursue more innovative and productive strategies. It is crucial to understand that technology in itself will enhance nothing. And even worse, it has the potential to perpetuate teaching and learning strategies that we long ago found to be ineffective. Specifically, I am talking about such things as (a) passive drill and practice activities, and (b) the use of computers without human contact and interaction. We have already discussed the importance of social discourse and how it relates to effective teaching and learning. My argument is not against technology, but against principals and teachers who allow technology to pull us backward.

I agree that technology has the potential to increase interactivity and social discourse; but it will only happen if principals as technology leaders and teachers insist on the appropriate use of technology in the classroom. G. Roger Sell (1996), from the University of Iowa, states this clearly:

> While technology can increase the potential for interactivity and social contact, it does not happen automatically. As with conventional classroom instruction, learning with technology can be isolating, encourage passivity on the part of the learner, and be void of authentic human contact. Provisions for involvement and feedback must be made in the design, development, implementation, and revision of programs using technology. (p. 12)

Pepi and Scheurman (1996), among many other researchers of technology implementation in schools, clearly state, "We conclude that as much reason exists to believe computer technology will reinforce and maintain the traditional role of the teacher as to believe it will become the agent for positive educational reform" (p. 232).

CONCLUDING THOUGHTS

The potential of technology presents both the greatest opportunity and the greatest threat to schools and their leaders. Successful principals as technology leaders will be those who decide to focus and concentrate on how best to intersect technology with teaching and learning.

Let me close with a few paradoxes we face as technology leaders:

1. Technology can improve the interaction and dialogue between teachers and students, resulting in improved teaching and learning, *but* it can also isolate, marginalize, and reduce effectiveness in the classroom.

2. Technology can offer its power to all students, *but* it can also segregate and deny that power.

3. Technology can assist with engaging students in meaningful learning and promote higher-level thinking, *but* it can also mirror traditional instructional pedagogy.

As I hope you agree, the answers do not lie in the hardware and software of our computer labs and classrooms. They are not disguised in workshops and conferences, nor evident in our university principal and teacher preparation programs. The answers lie with the technology leaders and teachers who will make the choices for the future.

If you stayed the course this far, you discovered that this book was not about hardware and software. The author's intent was to offer school principals and other school leaders some appropriate guidance as they face the immediate need to design, implement, manage, evaluate, and sustain effective technology programs to *significantly* affect teaching and student learning in the classroom. I hope my writing has been helpful.

The choice is in our hands: Do we put principals as technology leaders in the saddle, or let technology ride us?

CHAPTER TEN

OK, School Leaders, Let's Put One Together

A s I worked to prepare the final copy of this book, address-ing the suggestions/concerns of my reviewers, I realized something terribly important was missing: a final chapter focused on *how* the school leader puts the pieces of the puzzle together and actually *creates* effective technology programs around teaching and learning. Taking the suggestions of my reviewers seriously, I want to share a particular one with you:

> Yes, I agree the principal plays an important role. But I was hoping for more pages of "how." It is the same problem I have found while doing extensive research on implementing/ integrating technology into the curriculum. Everyone agrees that this needs to happen and can give multiple reasons "why" but there are few explanations of "how." The author has been very thorough in "why" but now let's see "how!"

The purpose in writing this book came back to me with a jolt. A need exists for a book to help school leaders plan and manage the use of technology in educational settings with student learn-ing and teacher development as the driving forces.

We have talked about Kaufman's SWOT analysis for several chapters, highlighting the three guiding questions:

1. Where do we want to go?
2. Why do we want to go there?
3. How will we know when we have arrived?

Focus with me for a moment on the second question: Why do we want to go there? You see, my reviewer has a point: As important as the why question is, the question of how is noticeably absent from our theoretical framework. I suggest Kaufman's model has one apparent weakness. It seems to cover all aspects of strategic planning except the how.

For the purposes of this chapter, and to draw attention to the importance of the how question, I take the liberty of providing an alternative second question: How will we get there? What follows is an example of a technology initiative whose planning team utilized this alternative question of how in the planning process.

THE PROBLEM

This story begins with the discussion among several public school principals and a couple of university faculty. Approximately 70% of the students classified as underachievers in Texas public schools come from minority populations. Consequently, many of these students drop out of school in the middle and high school years. The principals and university faculty had an overarching question: How can technology help us retain and reduce the dropout rate of low-achieving students? As you will see, their attempt to answer this question resulted in a program focused on *student learning and teacher development as the driving forces.*

TEXAS CENTER FOR ACADEMIC EXCELLENCE (TxCAE): A DISTANCE LEARNING INITIATIVE

Background

Sam Houston State University (SHSU), in participation with partnership sites—independent school districts, community organizations, and education service centers—established a technical assistance center that facilitates academic success and retention of underachievers in rural public schools. The Texas Center for Academic Excellence (TxCAE) is a comprehensive technical assistance agency designed to (a) structure a system to facilitate the diagnosis and prescription of underachievers to help them toward academic success, (b) establish a network of experts and successful programs, (c) structure a comprehensive professional development system to integrate disciplines (reading, language arts, mathematics, social studies, and science), and (d) maintain quality in the preparation of administrators, teachers, and community members.

Target students are those performing academically below grade level on the state testing program as determined by district measurable tools and the state criterion reference test. These students are also identified as below grade level due to factors such as (a) interrupted schooling, (b) limited language proficiency, (c) other home language, and/or (d) recent immigration.

The center is funded by a grant from the U.S. Department of Education and employs a director and two technology coordinators. Rather than simply purchasing technology equipment to service traditional needs, the focus of the program is on professional development for teachers and the application of technology to complement instruction. Specifically, the center maintains a computer-friendly technology Web page, where instructional lessons are housed. These lessons are developed by teachers in the field, who receive financial assistance from the center for their design and involvement in the program. To provide access to the online lessons at the TxCAE, students at the partnership schools are furnished with laptop computers (20 per participating site) for use at their school to link to the online lessons via the Internet.

For a complete description of the Texas Center for Academic Excellence, visit them online at http://www.shsu.edu/~txcae

TIME OUT: DECIDING ON WHERE WE WANT TO GO

Let's spend a few minutes setting up our SWOT analysis (recall Chapter 4). As I describe the process used by the TxCAE planning team, please think about your own technology plan in your education setting. The following statements outline the specific concerns the TxCAE group had as they attempted to answer the "Where do we want to go?" question.

1. Increase student pass rate on state criterion tests to 90%.

2. Eliminate students dropping out of school because they cannot be promoted due to low test scores.

3. Better address the needs of minority students, especially those with limited English skills and learning disabilities.

Recall our discussion earlier about those educators who spend enormous amounts of time and energy developing complex plans. Effective planning for technology focuses on where we want to go, justifies why we're headed in that direction, and makes it clear how we will know when we get there. The three statements above developed by the TxCAE planning team clearly and simply state where the principals and professors want to go. Your statements or questions should be just as specific and clear. OK, let's move on!

HOW WILL WE GET THERE?

Again, I encourage you to consider your own technology needs as we discuss how the TxCAE team will "get there." Be reminded that they designed their plan around two driving forces: (a) student learning and (b) teacher development. Staying focused on these two specific directions, the team kept their plan concise and directly related to where they wanted to go. Here are a few of their directions:

1. They secure written support and commitment to the program of each of the participating site principals and district superintendents.

2. The center personnel delivers professional development sessions to interested teachers and administrators, explaining the program in detail. These sessions demonstrate the process and procedure for creating lessons to be placed on the TxCAE Web site.

3. Teachers are paid to create instructional lessons and are paid to tutor students in after-school tutorials (this is an effective way to attract potential resisters and saboteurs to support the program).

4. The center technology coordinator travels to participating schools to assist teachers in the development and creation of online tutorial materials.

5. All participating students (and their parents) receive packets of introductory material with resources to facilitate communication and guidelines for using online curriculum resources.

Again, we see that the team's directions for "how we will get there" are pretty clear and straightforward. In addition, they directly address the two driving forces: student learning and professional development for teachers. Okay, on to the last piece of the puzzle!

HOW WILL WE KNOW WHEN WE ARRIVE?

Too often this step is either skipped or taken too lightly. Effective programs rarely result without attention paid to assessment and evaluation. Only through the use of multiple methods to measure student outcomes and teacher performance do we have a chance for continuous improvement.

The TxCAE team focuses on academic achievement, using both norm-referenced and criterion-referenced measures. Norm-referenced assessment information can be misleading in program evaluation because the tests do not assess program goals and typically measure outputs determined by state departments of education. To focus more on program inputs and outputs, criterion-referenced assessment information is used, consisting of objectives referencing, domain referencing, and minimum competency results.

The TxCAE team also utilizes other data sources that do not require objective test results. These sources include, but are not limited to, systematic observations and judgments of others (e.g., teachers, parents, and administrators) and secondary indicators of student performance (e.g., observation of students and student projects).

Alternative methods of assessment such as performance assessment, portfolio assessment, and assessment of affective characteristics are considered in the external evaluation of the program. In addition to the evaluation of knowledge and skills, the team considers affective characteristics of students such as appreciation, attitudes, interests, and values, as well as self-esteem and self-efficacy.

Annually, the TxCAE employs an external evaluator who conducts an analysis of the program and provides feedback on its effectiveness. This external evaluator analyzes data and develops a summative report to determine achievement of program goals and objectives.

NOW THE SWOT ANALYSIS

Though the TxCAE did not knowingly use the SWOT analysis, they did address the issues of *external and internal strengths, weaknesses, opportunities, and threats.* Without displaying a completed analysis, let me briefly describe some of these components in their program. Recall that Rebore's analysis process (see Table 4.1) involves a matrix consisting of three rows and four columns, focused on both external and internal strengths, weaknesses, opportunities, and threats. After identifying each of these components, an analysis is begun.

For example, the TxCAE recognized an internal strength to be the existence of two doctoral students within the College of Education, with experience and expertise in the design of instructional strategies using PowerPoint and Hyper Studio. In addition, the University Computer Center provided an external strength with graduate students outside the college offering assistance with Web-page design. The analysis of these two strengths resulted in financial compensation (through grant funds) for the students involved.

Let me close with one last example of how the TxCAE addressed an external weakness. The classroom teachers in the field, who are charged with designing instructional lessons to be placed on the student Web site, possessed limited expertise in using the appropriate hardware and software. However, they had the necessary classroom experience, as well as a good grounding in teaching and learning theory (external strength). The TxCAE planners needed to skillfully tie these two components together: the plan had to correct the external weakness while capitalizing on the strengths of the classroom teachers. The team's answer included doctoral students traveling to school sites to provide appropriate and relevant professional development to the teachers. Most important, however, was the plan's insistence on teachers themselves controlling the design of the instruction.

Remember our discussion in Chapter 4 about keeping technology plans simple and avoiding the tendency to create lengthy, complex, and highly technical plans. Your plan must be simple but effective, based on high-quality student outcomes, and built with a minimum of frustration and resistance. The TxCAE is such a plan—yours will be also.

Hopefully, this last chapter has accomplished my goal—to demonstrate the "how" of successful technology planning and implementation. I recommend a caution, however: The "how" can be quite situational, that is, it can depend on circumstances present in your own education setting. To illustrate, the TxCAE example discussed in this chapter was absent one of the most common *restraining, resisting, or discouraging forces* that affect change efforts with the implementation of technology: lack of funding. Other efforts and programs (maybe including your own) may not have the luxury of dollars from the U.S. Department of Education, so the plan in the example might not work for you. This draws attention to the need to not follow a set of blueprints created by someone else. Only your planning team knows the needs of your education setting and the existence of certain driving forces as well as restraining forces.

Speaking of funding, any school administrator in need of grant funds should immediately become familiar with the *No Child Left Behind Act*, which Congress approved in December 2001. This act provides billions of dollars for schools to address the improvement of academic achievement. School districts all across the country are encouraged to seek funding through this promising program.

CONCLUSION

Allow me to reference one last piece of work in our concluding discussion of *The Principal as Technology Leader:* Kurt Lewin's (1951) book entitled *Field Theory in Social Science.* In discussing the change process, he suggests any change or movement from an existing level of performance to a desired level of performance involves two different kinds of forces: (a) driving or encouraging forces and (b) restraining, resisting, or discouraging forces. We earlier talked about the importance of including the resisters and saboteurs in our planning for technology. But the question haunts us: Is it better to increase the driving forces or decrease the restraining forces? I suppose the answer is both. However, we have a long history in educational leadership of spending all of our time trying to increase the driving forces, resulting in very short-lived spurts of success. My hunch is that ignoring the restraining forces serves to build or expand the resistance from the resisters and saboteurs. Unless the resisters are included in some way, the driving forces can often be stopped in their tracks. In many organizations, especially schools, it is much more difficult to implement change than it is to maintain the status quo. With the restraining forces still in place, the tendency exists to quickly return to the former level of performance.

Although I possess a passionate belief in the potential of technology to truly improve teaching and learning, I also find myself questioning our misguided expectation that technology will not only get us where we want to go, but will do so ahead of schedule. I am not convinced that technology by itself will accomplish anything: Actually, I argue that by itself, it becomes a barrier and detriment to good teaching and effective learning. Somewhere within our reach is the realization that we must keep our focus on what we know about good teaching, the importance of leadership, and leaving no child behind. Expecting technology to be the answer is putting the cart before the horse. Technology by itself will not get us where we want to go. It must be driven by teachers and students using technology as a tool to perform at a higher level.

Resource A:
A SWOT Matrix
for Technology
Planning

	Strengths	Weaknesses	Opportunities	Threats
Internal data				
External data				
Analysis				

Note: Credit is given for the SWOT Matrix to Roger Kaufman (1998), University of Florida.

Resource B: Administrative Dimensions and Look-Fors

Planning—Defines purpose and sets organizational goals

- Seeks clarity in purpose and goal setting in various activities
- Utilizes planning and goal setting to advance organizational mission
- Clarifies the purpose and goals of various activities
- Encourages staff in planning and goal accomplishment
- Links planning to goal accomplishment

Organizing—Defines tasks to be completed in various activities

- Outlines tasks to be completed
- Arranges tasks to be accomplished in sequential order
- Breaks larger tasks into smaller, manageable activities
- Defines clearly the tasks to be completed
- Visualizes constraints inhibiting task accomplishment

Problem solving—Analyzes problems effectively and reaches logical conclusions

- Defines the problem logically before formulating a course of action
- Identifies important elements of a problem prior to reaching a decision
- Seeks to frame the problem in context before reaching a conclusion

- Collects and analyzes essential information before reaching a conclusion
- Clarifies the problem with others before drawing a conclusion

Creativity—Demonstrates innovation and inventiveness in work-related situations

- Suggests innovative means to reach specific ends
- Provides innovative suggestions to faculty and staff in handling educational issues
- Encourages innovative and unique alternatives for handling difficult issues
- Suggests innovative means to accomplish organizational objectives
- Stimulates creative thought by modeling innovative thinking

Decisiveness—Renders timely, appropriate decisions, and accepts the consequences

- Reaches decisions logically and in a timely fashion
- Distinguishes between urgent decisions and those that can be postponed
- Deciphers issues on the basis of information needed to render a decision
- Makes a decision if appropriate information is available
- Demonstrates reasonable caution in timing the decision

Systems analysis—Understands educational systems in the effective functioning of operational components

- Understands the function of educational systems
- Holds a mental image of how the various elements must complement each other
- Analyzes subsystems for effective operation
- Possesses wide-ranging knowledge of organizational subsystems
- Encourages the faculty and staff to invest in systems thinking

Vision—Possesses a clear and positive view of the past, present, and future of the school

- Possesses and models the vision of an ideal school
- Interprets school vision and practices to the school community
- Seeks to develop and continually modify a shared vision of the school
- Challenges norms that undermine the educational vision
- Maintains a student-centered vision for the school

Communications—Processes messages with precise understanding

- Conveys opinions succinctly and appropriately when communicating
- Expresses clear and concise language in communiqués
- Checks for understanding when communicating
- Uses appropriate communication modes
- Uses language appropriate to the situation

Instructional leadership—Works effectively with the school community to advance student learning

- Emphasizes instructional leadership within the school community
- Encourages teacher participation on instructional issues
- Conducts frequent, formative teacher evaluations
- Articulates high expectations for student achievement
- Serves as a resource for teacher reflection on instructional issues

Group leadership and team building—Mobilizes others to collaborate in accomplishing school goals and solving problems

- Uses knowledge appropriate to enhancing group dynamics
- Facilitates group consensus and synergy
- Promotes mutually developed group goals and objectives
- Establishes a framework for collaborative group action
- Recognizes when the group needs direction and intervention

Climate development—Shapes the psychosocial environment of the school to promote accomplishment of the mission

- Ensures a safe environment for learning
- Works effectively with diverse elements of the school community

- Attends to elements of the physical environment to maximize student learning
- Maintains a facilitative psychological and social environment
- Encourages and values contributions of all stakeholders

Moral responsibility—Demonstrates universally held core values and beliefs

- Models universally held values and beliefs to students, staff, and community
- Sets and maintains high standards of moral development
- Upholds the dignity of all stakeholders
- Clarifies expectations on a set of clear and consistent values
- Upholds professional and legal responsibilities

References

Achilles, C. (2001). The intellectual firepower needed for educational administration's new era of enlightenment. In P. Jenlick (Ed.), *21st century challenges for school administrators* (pp. 89-100). Lanham, MD: Scarecrow Press.

Andersen, H. C. (1949). *The emperor's new clothes*. New York: Harper.

Avolio, B. J. (2000). *Full leadership development: Building the vital forces in organizations*. London: Sage.

Barth, R. S. (1990). *Improving schools from within*. San Francisco: Jossey-Bass.

Bolman, L., & Deal, T. (1997). *Reframing organizations*. San Francisco: Jossey-Bass.

Brooks, J. G., & Brooks, M. G. (1993). Becoming a constructivist teacher. In *In search of understanding: The case for constructivist classrooms* (pp. 103-118). Washington, DC: Association for Supervision and Curriculum Development.

Callister, T. A., & Dunne, F. (1992). The computer as doorstop: Technology as disempowerment. *Phi Delta Kappan, 74*(4), 324-326.

Center for Research on Information Technology and Organizations. (1998). *Teaching, learning, and computing 1998—A study of teachers' use of computer technology, their pedagogies, and their school context*. University of California, Irvine.

Champy, J. A. (1996). *Reengineering management: The mandate for new leadership*. New York: Harper Business.

Coleman, D. (2001). Administrative skills vs. achievement standards as predictors of administrative success. In P. Jenlick (Ed.), *21st century challenges for school administrators* (pp. 53-64). Lanham, MD: Scarecrow Press.

Creighton, T. (1999). Idaho technology leadership center. *Society for Information Technology & Teacher Education, 1*(1), 444-449.

Cuban, L. (2001). *Oversold and underused: Computers in the classroom.* Cambridge, MA: Harvard University Press.

Davis, S. (1998). Superintendents' perspectives on the involuntary departure of public school principals: The most frequent reasons why principals lose their jobs. *Educational Administration Quarterly, 34*(1), 58-90.

English, F. (2000). Looking behind the veil: Addressing the enigma of educational leadership. *Education Leadership Review, 1*(3), 1-7.

Fine, L. (2001, May 10). Special needs gap. *Education Week*, p. 26.

Fosnot, C. T. (1993). Rethinking science education: A defense of Piagetian Constructivism. *Journal of Research in Science Teaching, 30*(9), 1189-1201.

Fullan, M. (2001). *Leading in a culture of change.* San Francisco: Jossey-Bass.

Gehring, J. (2001, May 10). Not enough girls. *Education Week*, p. 18.

Gerstner, L. (1994). *Reinventing education: Entrepreneurship in today's schools.* New York: E. P. Hutton.

Glatthorn, A. A. (1995). *Quality teaching through professional development.* Thousand Oaks, CA: Corwin.

Glickman, C. (1998). *Supervision of instruction: A developmental approach.* Needham Heights, MA: Allyn & Bacon.

Goodlad, J. (1997). *Public purpose of education and schooling.* San Francisco: Jossey-Bass.

Hoyle, J. (2001). I've got standards, you've got standards, all God's children got standards. *AASA Professor, 24*(2), 27-32.

Johnson, R. J. (2001, May 10). Money matters. *Education Week*, pp. 14-15.

Jones, B. F., Valdez, G., Nowakowski, J., & Rasmussen, C. (1995). *Plugging in: Choosing and using educational technology.* Oak Brook, IL: North Central Regional Laboratory.

Kaufman, R., Herman, J., & Watters, K. (1998). *Educational planning: Strategic, tactical, operational.* Lancaster, PA: Technomic Press.

Kendall, J. S., & Marzano, R. J. (2001). *Content knowledge: A compendium of standards and benchmarks for K-12 education* (3rd ed.). Aurora, CO: Mid-continent Regional Education Laboratory and the Association for Supervision and Curriculum Development.

Kennedy Manzo, K. (2001, May 10). Academic record. *Education Week*, p. 22.

Knezek, D. (2001). *Technology standards for school administrators.* Naperville, IL: North Central Regional Technology in Education Consortium.

Lemke, C. (1998). *Technology in American schools: Seven dimensions for gauging progress.* Santa Monica, CA: Milken Family Foundation.

Lewin, K. (1951). *Field theory in social science: Selected theoretical papers* (D. Cartwright, Ed.). New York: Harper.

Lumley, D. (1993). *Planning for technology: A guidebook for school administrators.* New York: Scholastic.

Maurer, R. (1996). *Beyond the wall of resistance: Unconventional strategies that build support for change.* New York: Bard Press.

Meyer, L. (2001, May 10). New challenges. *Education Week*, pp. 49-54.

Moss Kanter, R. (2001). *Evolve: Succeeding in the digital culture of tomorrow.* Boston: Harvard Business School Press.

Murphy, J. (1997). *The landscape of leadership preparation: Reframing the education of school administrators.* Thousand Oaks, CA: Corwin.

Nicaise, M., & Barnes, D. (1996). The union of technology, constructivism, and teacher education. *Journal of Teacher Education, 47*(3), 205-212.

Office of Technology Assessment. (1988). *Power on! New tools for teaching and learning.* Washington, DC: Government Printing Office.

Office of Technology Assessment. (1989). *Teachers and technology: Making the connection.* Washington, DC: Government Printing Office.

Office of Technology Assessment. (1995). *Linking for learning: A new source for education.* Washington, DC: Government Printing Office.

Pepi, D., & Scheurman, G. (1996). The emperor's new computer: A critical look at our appetite for technology. *Journal of Teacher Education, 47*(3), 229-236.

Peters, T., & Waterman, R. (1982). *In search of excellence.* New York: HarperCollins.

Piaget, J. (1969). *Psychology of the child.* New York: Basic books.

Quinn-Mills, R. (2001). *E-leadership: Guiding your business to success in the new economy.* Englewood Cliffs, NJ: Prentice Hall.

Rebore, R. (1998). *Personnel administration in education: A management approach.* Needham Heights, MA: Allyn & Bacon.

Richie, D. (1996). The administrative role in the integration of technology. *NASSP Bulletin, 12*(1), 42-51.

Richie, D., & Rodriquez, S. (1997). The role of technology in school leadership. *Journal of Information Technology for Teacher Education, 1*(1), 111-124.

Ringle, M., & Updegrove, D. (1998). Is strategic planning for technology an oxymoron? *Cause–Effect, 21*(1), 18-23.

Robbins, R. (1982). *Personnel: The management of human resources* (2nd ed.). Englewood Cliffs, NJ: Prentice Hall.

Sarason, S. (1997). *How schools might be governed and why.* New York: Teachers College Press.

Schlechty, P. (1997). *Inventing better schools: An action plan for educational reform.* San Francisco: Jossey-Bass.

Sell, G. R. (1996). *Technology implementation.* Unpublished manuscript, University of Iowa, Iowa City.

Senge, P. (1996). *The fifth discipline: The art and practice of the learning organization.* New York: Doubleday/Currency.

Sergiovani, T. (1996). *Leadership for the schoolhouse.* San Francisco: Jossey-Bass.

Smith, R. E. (1998). *Human resources administration: A school-based perspective.* Larchmont, NY: Eye on Education.

Technology Standards for School Administrators Collaborative. (2001). Naperville, IL: North Central Regional Technology in Education Consortium.

U.S. Department of Education's National Commission on Excellence in Education. (1983). *A nation at risk.* Washington, DC: U.S. Department of Education.

Vaill, P. (1998). *Spirited leading and learning.* San Francisco: Jossey-Bass.

Vygotsky, L. S. (1962). *Thought and language* (E. Hanfmann & G. Vakar, Eds. & Trans.). Cambridge: MIT Press.

Index

CORWIN PRESS

The Corwin Press logo—a raven striding across an open book—represents the happy union of courage and learning. We are a professional-level publisher of books and journals for K-12 educators, and we are committed to creating and providing resources that embody these qualities. Corwin's motto is "Success for All Learners."